EVER WONDERED WHY?

A STUDENT'S GUIDE TO 81 SCIENTIFIC MARVELS

SIDDHARTHA BANDYOPADHYAY

INDIA • SINGAPORE • MALAYSIA

ISBN
Paperback 979-8-89610-702-6
Hardcase 979-8-89632-462-1

Dedicated to

My teachers at The Heritage School, Kolkata who inspired me to recognize the deep connection between science and our everyday lives and my Sir , Mr Ushnish Sangiri who held me strongly as I stood at the cross-roads of a career choice.

Acknowledgement

I thank the Almighty for blessing me with the opportunity to present this book to my readers.

I am deeply honored by the support of His Excellency, Dr. C. V. Ananda Bose IAS, Hon'ble Governor of West Bengal who graciously reviewed my manuscript and penned the Foreword. Your blessings mean the world to me.

I am profoundly grateful to my mentors at The Heritage School—Principal Mrs. Seema Sapru, Headmaster Mr Darryl C Christensen and Headmistress Mrs. Runa Chatterjee—whose years of guidance and nurture, sparked my intellectual curiosity and shaped my perspective on science and life.

It was an exciting journey, made possible with the unwavering support and encouragement of my parents Dr Saugata Bandyopadhyay and Dr Rajashree Ray, who inspired me from an early age and believed in my potential.

To my younger brother, Aniruddha, thank you for your infinite patience, understanding, and for being a constant sounding board throughout this process.

Gratitude to my friends in school with whom I paired up for quizzes, science and mathematics competitions and projects for years, which kept the flame of curiosity alive in me.

I owe a debt of gratitude to my mother for drawing the illustrations painstakingly to enhance the appeal of the book and aid to clarify the complex ideas in a young reader's mind.

Working with the exceptional team at Notion Press has been an absolute privilege, and I thank each of you for your dedication, expertise, and hard work in bringing this project to life.

Author's Biography

Siddhartha is a 19-year-old student, pursuing an Integrated Master of Physics Course at University of Oxford, UK. He passed Indian School Certificate Examinations (Class 12) in 2023 from The Heritage School, Kolkata, India. He was the School Vice-Captain and represented India at the Asia Pacific Forum for Science Talented in Taiwan in 2019. He was awarded with the NTSE and KVPY scholarships-both prestigious national-level scholarships in India for outstanding students and won the Quadsparks Competition in IISc, Bangalore in 2022. He is a member of Mensa Indian arm of the International High IQ society Mensa.

An avid quizzer, with numerous national and regional laurels in GK and science and mathematics quizzes, a passionate musician, with a Grade 8 certificate in Violin from the ABRSM, UK, he enjoys sports, holds a Black Belt in Karate, a FIDE-rating in Chess and has joined the rowing club in his college.

A writer from a young age, he was the Editor of the Science magazine in school and published his first e-book of poems and short stories, "Through my Pencil's Lens" in 2022. Fascinated from a young age by the mysteries of stars and black holes, he aspires to build a career in astrophysics and quantum physics.

Contents

राज्यपाल, पश्चिम बंगाल
Governor of West Bengal
রাজ্যপাল, পশ্চিমবঙ্গ

Foreword

Everyday science every man's science

Reminiscent of Siddhartha of yore becoming enlightened under the Bodhi tree, here is Siddhartha Bandyopadhyay creating a Bodhi tree of scientific knowledge for the enlightenment of curious young readers." Sidhartha Bandyopadhyay's ' Ever wondered why' is an absorbing and enriching journey into the world of science, dovetailed to the requirements of the inquisitive young readers. It demystifies scientific marvels that puzzles in the minds of novitiate learners. Through its lucid language and structured approach, the author not only stimulates curiosity but also provides answers to the questions that arise in the minds of inquisitive readers.

The book is meticulously crafted with each chapter revolving around a specific scientific question such as, 'Why does the moon appear to change shape" or "What causes seasons". This question-based approach ignites the readers' curiosity, stimulating the insightful tendencies of young minds. The book promotes critical thinking and eggs on the students to ponder over the underlying mechanism of the Universe we live in. Bandyopadhyay's writing style is marked by seamless clarity. He simplifies complex concepts without compromising on depth each chapter starts with a captivating introduction, followed by a detailed explanation."

'Ever wondered why' delves into multi disciplinary realms of science, including physics, chemistry, biology and environmental science. The book thus presents the interconnectedness of different fields and conveys the idea that science is a cohesive body of knowledge. While analysing the phenomenon of rainbow, the author elaborates on light refraction and reflection and touches upon the cultural significance of rainbows. This holistic view pervades the entire work. The book also deals with contemporary issues such as climate change and appeals to the readers to realise their roles in the shape of things to come on our planet.

The illustrations in the book add value to the work and enhance its appeal. Visual aids clarify complex ideas and enhance the reader's comprehension. They make a content more engaging.

The fun facts and trivia spices up the book and enhances its readability as interesting titbits. Bandyopadhyay emphasizes that science is not just static facts but a dynamic process of inquiry and discovery.

Furthermore, Bandyopadhyay's emphasis on environmental issues resonates strongly in today's contexts. He addresses topics like global warming and biodiversity, encouraging readers to recognize their social responsibility toward the planet".

"Ever wondered why-a student's guide to 81 scientific marvel", is a commendable resource for the readers who want to explore the mystery of science. Siddhartha Bandyopadhyay has crafted a book that masterfully balances lucidity and depth ,simplifying abstruse scientific concepts, making them easily accessible to what Virginia Woolf calls, 'The common reader'.

An examination of the various articles ,will throw light on the depth of its content and beauty of the presentation. The article, 'Understanding the air conditioning and temperature regulation', clarifies why the air-conditioners are kept high on ceiling, following the principles of convection, warm air rises and cool air sinks and a higher location optimizes cooling efficiency.

Condensation in cars '-This article explains why car windows fog up when the A/C is working.The concept of condensation is the fact of the matter. The article explains how humidity and temperature interact to create droplets on the glass. Car engine mechanics - How cars start when a key is turned, is a common man doubt .This article explains the concept of ignition process with clarity. Fatigues and eye bags-why do we develop dark circles, when we are tired? Fluid build up, skin thickness and circulation are explained in this article with biological and physiological concepts.

Milton says "A good book is precious life blood of a master spirit." That is about the creation of a book . Once the book becomes a reality , Virginia Woolf' Common Reader ' takes over . How does he respond to a book? That depends on the quality of the book. Francis Bacon places books into three categories:" Some books are to be tasted , others to be swallowed and some few to be chewed and digested." Irrespective of its classification, this book "ever, will remain as a salubrious presence in the minds of the reading public. Well done, Sri Siddhartha Bandyopadhyay. 'Tomorrow to fresh woods and pastures anew."

Kolkata

His Excellency Dr C V Ananda Bose, IAS
Governor of West Bengal

About the Author

Mrs Seema Sapru
Principal, The Heritage School

Siddhartha is the kind of child every parent and teacher would dream of. From the very beginning of his time at our school, he has exemplified the qualities of a perfect gentleman. Originally coming back to India from the UK, Siddhartha faced some initial challenges in adjusting to life at The Heritage School—differences in accent and culture made the transition a bit daunting. However, with the unwavering support of his parents, both of whom are doctors, he and his brother Aniruddha quickly adapted and became well-liked by their peers.

Siddhartha has always been a bright and inquisitive student. He displayed exceptional intelligence and a natural curiosity, qualities that made him stand out. He took great initiative, particularly in science-related activities, while also nurturing a passion for literature. As he grew up within The Heritage School, Siddhartha took on various leadership roles, including Assistant Prefect, Prefect, and a member of the student council. His contributions were not just limited to these roles; he actively inspired his peers through his dedication and enthusiasm.

An integral part of the STEM Club, Siddhartha set his sights on ambitious academic goals, aiming for institutions like Cambridge and Oxford. Through hard work and determination, he achieved admission to his dream program in Astrophysics and Computer Science. Even after securing this milestone, Siddhartha maintained a deep connection with his school. Before heading to Oxford, he returned to teach math and science to students across various classes. His teaching was marked by his commitment to excellence and his ability to engage young minds.

One of Siddhartha's defining traits is his insatiable curiosity. He would often pose challenging and thought-provoking questions, some of which even left his teachers stumped! His mother, Dr. Rajashree Ray, has been a constant pillar of support, balancing her career, family, and her children's education with remarkable grace. She has played a crucial role in ensuring Siddhartha and his brother had the best possible upbringing, encompassing academics, co-curricular activities, and a well-rounded lifestyle.

Siddhartha's love for quizzing further highlighted his keen intellect. He formed a strong bond with our quiz trainer and consistently excelled in competitions. Despite his many achievements, Siddhartha remained grounded and approachable, endearing himself to everyone around him. In his school days, he was a happy-go-lucky child, unconcerned about weight management or appearances, focusing instead on his studies and activities. However, when he went to Oxford, he embraced a more disciplined lifestyle, returning as a confident, fit, and charismatic young man.

His connection with the school continues, as he regularly judges various events, from science and robotics competitions to literary programs. Always cheerful and willing to contribute, Siddhartha brings his trademark innocent smile and positive disposition to every interaction.

Today, I feel honored to write the foreword for his book. Siddhartha is not only academically brilliant but also flexible, resilient, and resourceful—qualities that will undoubtedly ensure his success in life. While he may not be overly meticulous in some aspects, he exemplifies adaptability and creativity, always ready with multiple backup plans. His multifaceted personality ensures that he thrives regardless of the challenges he faces.

I believe this is only the beginning of his journey as an author. Siddhartha writes beautifully, and I am confident this book will not be his last. Wishing him all the best for a bright and fulfilling future! I hope that one day, even after I have retired, I will have the joy of seeing him again. God bless you, Siddhartha!

Book Review

Mr Darryl Christopher Christensen
Headmaster, The Heritage School

I met Siddhartha when he was in class six, leading a team of three students in a quiz that was being conducted at our school. Sid, as he was better known, stated in his clipped British accent, "I know we are not going to win." He could have become a soothsayer, as true enough, our school came third. Needless to say, Sid, along with a few highly talented and motivated friends, dominated the quizzing circuit for the next few years. In class twelve, he led the school quiz club as its president, winning multiple laurels. As a very soft-spoken, honest, and intelligent young person, Sid is someone who speaks in very simple, precise language, articulating his thoughts clearly without hesitation or bias.

I have found myself listening to him on multiple occasions, absolutely fascinated by his command over multiple topics and thoroughly enjoying his company.

While reading through his writing, I was again transported to my office sofa, where he, seated alongside, was speaking to me in his thoroughly delightful accent.

The questions Sid covers are simple daily facts that we often take for granted and brush under the carpet. Each question has been addressed using clear, lucid language and is kept brief to prevent attention from drifting.Scientific terminology, where necessary, has been treated with care to avoid overwhelming a young mind, while still giving it due importance.

The why's and how's that often clutter the minds of children find clarity without delving into details that might be daunting.Sid explains things in a way as if he were having a conversation with someone, not delivering a boring lecture. Thus, he has the ability to grasp and hold the attention of a reader.

Sid comes across as a person who is wise beyond his years, yet still young enough to resemble a high school student. I have known Sid for over nine years and have developed a close relationship with him. I wish him all the very best in his future career.

Mr Darryl Christopher Christensen
Headmaster, The Heritage School

Book Review

Mrs Runa Chatterjee
Headmistress, The Heritage School

Ever- wondered - why' has focussed on certain things which catch our attention, spark our curiosity, or make us ponder about certain day – to – day complexities of life? This book is a journey into those questions that have danced on the edges of our minds, begging for answers and inviting deeper contemplation.

When you delve into this book, you'll find yourself navigating through a labyrinth of intriguing inquiries and captivating explorations. Each topic is a testament to the human spirit's unquenchable thirst for knowledge and understanding. The author, with a keen eye for detail and a profound sense of wonder, has meticulously compiled and addressed questions that span the breadth of human experience.

The charm of this book lies not just in the questions it poses, but in the thoughtful and insightful answers it provides. Whether you're a casual reader or a seasoned scholar, you'll find yourself nodding in agreement, raising an eyebrow in surprise, and most importantly, feeling a connection to the universal quest for knowledge.

As you turn the pages, you'll encounter questions that may have lingered at the back of your mind for years, alongside new curiosities that will pique your interest. The journey is both enlightening and enjoyable, inviting you to pause, reflect, and maybe even share a knowing smile as you uncover the 'whys' of the world around you.

Being a lover of music, the questions based on the working of the violin, guitar, piano and drums fascinated me. The answer to the question… "What makes a song sound good" really clarified my understanding of the complex interplay of the factors that result in the enjoyment of music.

In a world that often rushes past the small wonders, this book is a gentle reminder to slow down and savor the questions that make us human. It invites you to embrace curiosity, celebrate discovery, and join the timeless pursuit of wisdom. So, dear reader, open your mind and let your curiosity lead the way. **Ever wondered why' is not just a collection of answers, but a celebration of the questions that define our existence.

Happy reading!

Mrs Runa Chatterjee
Headmistress, The Heritage School

Prologue

I remember the day, less than a decade ago, when I turned 11 years. I was reading about blackholes in Carl Sagan's 'Cosmos', gifted by my parents on my birthday. Lost in the pages of the book, I would look at the night sky and marvelled at how fascinating the space was.

That was the moment when my curiosity about space, science, and the unknown began to flood my young mind. As I grew up, it appeared that science was at work in everyday tasks we undertook, from the bedroom to the classroom.

Through concepts like motion, forces, chemical reactions, and energy, science explained everyday phenomena such as walking, driving a car, cooking in a microwave, or using a phone.

Throughout my school years, I was fortunate to have teachers who fuelled my quest for knowledge, giving me opportunities to explore, fail, and succeed.. More than textbooks, I learnt from stories and fictional documentaries by authors and scientists, who simplified the intriguing complexities of scientific phenomenon, by relating them to our everyday experiences.

From questions in quantum physics to architecture, engineering, acoustics, electrodynamics, music, geology, and medical diagnostics, science lays the foundation for understanding it all. As I enjoyed observing patterns and connecting the extraordinary science behind everyday events, I wished there was a book at my level of understanding, as a high school student, to guide me. I spent hours searching for answers to the mysteries behind the astonishing invisible forces around us. For me, science was about understanding how it makes our modern world so convenient, not just an abstract concept defined by black holes and gravity waves.

When I finished school, I promised my younger friends I would write a book that brings everyday scientific concepts to life." I want every student to be curious about the world around us, to notice the events happening every day, and to understand how the universe operates in harmony through forces, reactions, and interactions. As you read this book, you will be able to relate to the gadgets you operate everyday, to the senses and perceptions that you experience and many more topics that interest you . You will understand why it is more fun to play than study, why we blow on the cup of hot coffee, how water originated from space and many more interesting facts.

I chose 81 topics because this number has significant connections to science. It's 9 x 9 in mathematics, the atomic number of thallium in chemistry, the dielectric constant of pure water in physics, and Messier 81 is Bode's galaxy.

I hope you enjoy reading this book and come to appreciate the principles of science in your life. Here's to number 81!

Siddhartha Bandyopadhyay

1

Why are air conditioners placed near the ceiling and not on the ground?

The answer lies in a concept we learned as kids: hot air rises, and cold air sinks!! When a gas is heated, its molecules become more energetic and move faster and faster, whizzing around all over the place. As a result, the gas becomes thinner and lighter, rising above the cold air. This continuous cycle, known as convection, helps balance the overall temperature of the air Now, when we want to cool down a room, we'll need to be efficient and cool down the hot air. After all, there's no point in cooling the cold air if the hot air remains!" That's why the air conditioner is installed near the ceiling, where it can cool the hot air first.

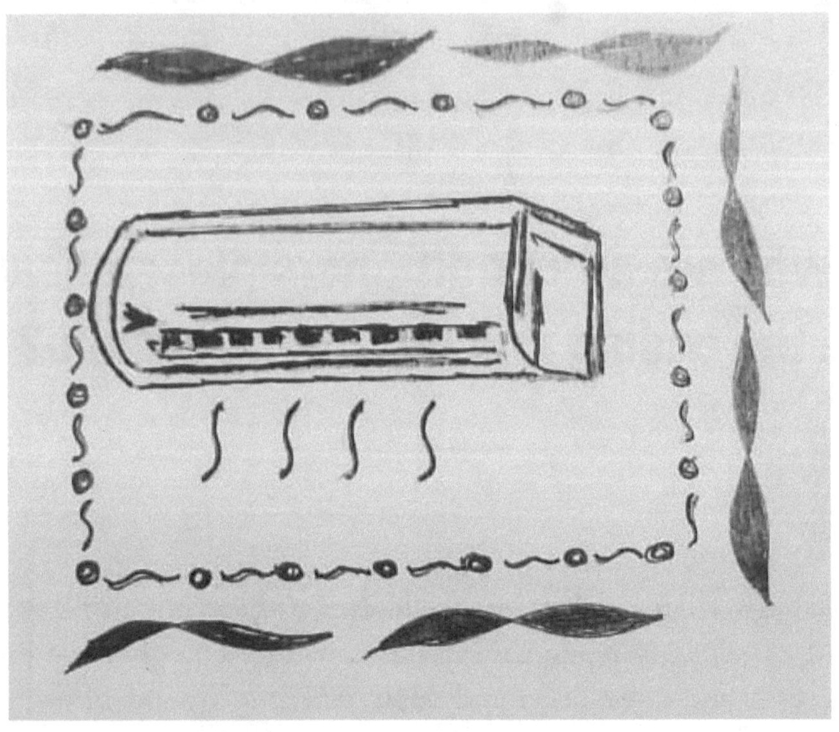

AC Machine

2

Why do the windows fog up when the AC inside the car is on?

You've probably noticed that after running the AC for a while, the car windows turn cloudy. Sometimes, you'll even see water droplets forming and running down the windows. This fog and the droplets are caused by water vapor in the air turning into liquid! Through a process called condensation, gas transforms into liquid when the temperature is low enough. Here, the hot humid air outside the car meets the cool window. The water vapor condenses into liquid. Depending on certain conditions, it either forms mist or droplets.

When the air is quite humid and cools down quickly, the droplets remain 'suspended' or mixed in the air, forming a mist. If the air isn't that humid, the vapour will turn into the droplets that run down your window.

You might be wondering why other gases don't condense. After all, air is also made window simply isn't cold enough! These other gases require very, very low temperatures to condense – temperatures our AC would never be able to produce

Car AC Machine

3

How does a car start when the key is turned?

Cars, like most other modes of transportation, run on engines, which are powerful sources of energy. By manipulating hot air and fuel (in an internal combustion engine), the car gains enough energy to move. When you turn the car key, the ignition switch activates and starts the electrical system.. After that, an electrical signal is sent to the starter motor, which helps crank the engine (a motor is an electrical device that rotates gears in all kinds of machines).

To understand what goes on inside the engine, we will first need to understand its components. The engine consists mainly of pistons and valves. Pistons are small metallic cylinders that move up and down to create motion, while valves control the flow of air in the engine.

Now that we're clear with the components, let's look at the procedure. The first step is the intake stroke. The intake valve opens to allow an air-fuel mixture into the engine's cylinders, while the piston moves down to create a vacuum that sucks the mixture in. Next comes the compression stroke. The piston moves back up, compressing the mixture. This increases the temperature and pressure, making it easier to ignite. Once the piston reaches the top, the combustion stroke starts. The spark plug, that provides an electric spark, sets the mixture on fire. The explosion pushes the piston back down, generating enough energy to rotate the wheels. Finally, the valve opens again, during the exhaust stroke, and the burnt mixture is allowed to leave.

But how do the wheels rotate? Well, the piston is connected to a crankshaft, which rotates the gears. This motion is what allows the car to move.

A simple turn of the key brings an intricate system to life, propelling us to our destination!

Car Ignition

4

Why do we get eye bags when we feel tired?

It turns out that eye bags, or the dark circles around our eyes, result from several factors. However, it is mostly due to the build-up of fluid under them. When interstitial fluid (the fluid around cells) builds up under our eyes, it causes swelling and puffiness.

Additionally, the skin under the eyes is thinner than in other areas, making signs of fatigue more visible. When we are tired, this effect becomes more noticeable. The skin thins further and becomes more delicate due to dehydration and reduced collagen production—a protein that gives skin strength, structure, and elasticity.. Without hydration and collagen, the blood vessels beneath the skin and underlying structures become increasingly visible, creating this darkened appearance.

Fatigue also reduces blood circulation, causing blood to pool under the eyes.. Once again, this causes the blood vessels to be more pronounced, leading to a bluish tinge (just like the veins on your arms and hands). Finally, chronic (long-standing) fatigue and stress may trigger an increased production of melanin. Melanin is a pigment that influences the colour of our skin and protects us from the harmful UV rays of the Sun.

Eye bag formation

The more melanin your body has, the darker the skin is. When our body produces an excess of melanin, because of fatigue and stress, the effect becomes highly visible in areas with thin skin.

Now you might ask, why is the skin below our eyes so thin? The answer to that is also multilayered. Firstly, there is less fat around the eyes, and the muscles (orbicularis oculi) present are quite thin. More importantly, our face makes a variety of expressions to convey our emotions, and to enable this, the skin on the face must be stretchy and thin. All these factors combined, result in the thin skin below our eyes.

5

Why do our fingers and nose go red when it's cold?

Before we dive into the answer, let's solve this together! What's the first thing your body does when it's cold? That's right—it tries to keep you warm! It will stop as much heat as it can from escaping. Can you think of any ways it would do this? It can't simply turn on a heater inside your stomach, can it?

I'll give you a hint: there's a reason we are called warm-blooded animals!

To prevent the loss of heat, our body manipulates the blood vessels in an interesting way. To keep our vital organs warm, the first thing it does is constrict the blood flow to the extremities – our fingertips, nose and toes. It quite literally squeezes the blood vessels to stop the flow. This process, known as vasoconstriction, allows for more blood to circulate about the vital organs, keeping them warm. However, restricting blood flow for too long is harmful—that's how frostbite occurs! So, the body reopens the vessels and allows blood to flow once more(called vasodilation). This sudden rush of blood back into the extremities causes the reddish color we often see, especially in the nose, where blood vessels are closer to the surface.

The Red Nose

6

How does Google seem to know everything?

To understand Google, we'll first need to learn about the world wide web and the internet!

The World Wide Web is undeniably the backbone of modern society."Answers at the tips of our fingers, access to unbridled information, communication across the globe; these are but few of the blessings W3 (world wide web) has granted us. By design, it seems so intricate, delicate and complex, like the spider's web it's named after. Yet, if we dig deeper, the concept becomes far simpler and as clear as crystal.

First, let's redefine our notion of the internet. The internet is merely a communication device. It allows us to share things. You might ask, what things? Well, pretty much everything. Files in the form of documents, images, videos, and audio make up the information you're searching for.. Wikipedia is simply a collection of these documents, YouTube and Netflix are collections of these videos and audios, and Instagram is primarily a collection of these images. Evidently, virtual information is received and perceived in the form files. It is the internet which allows us to share and access them.

Think of the internet like a virtual postal service - Digital Royal Mail. Every computer connected to it has an address, just like a house.". This address is known as an IP (Internet Protocol) address. When you connect to the internet through an ISP (Internet Service Provider, like Vodafone, Jio, AT&T, etc.), your computer is assigned one of these IP addresses.

Unfortunately, the storeroom of our virtual Royal Mail is a mess. We need a good way of organizing it. That's where the World Wide Web comes in. W3 acts as the medium which sorts the vast collection of documents into filing cabinets. It assigns a naming system to each website and webpage through an address. This is the layer where information resides. It has a very intricate way of assigning the location of each of these documents. Through several protocols (rules of the internet) it accesses them when called upon.

However, we still aren't done! It's no good having all the webpages and websites neatly organised in lockers, but unable to be retrieved! We need a good mailman to deliver the mail to us. That's where Google and other such search engines come in. Google helps deliver a choice assortment of websites when we ask for certain keywords...like an all-you-can-eat buffet. You are not sure whether you want kung-

pao chicken or chilli fish, but you are sure you want Chinese food. In the same way, you enter a general keyword into Google, and using its complex algorithm, it will find a host of relevant websites. It will search all the file cabinets of the world wide web and deliver the relevant documents to your doorstep.

Google - the Master of all ?

7

How do aeroplanes fly?

Aeroplanes are truly a wonder of machinery. These gigantic metal contraptions soar through the sky—so why doesn't their weight pull them down? Let's find out.

The atmosphere around us is actually quite heavy, with layers of air stretching almost 100 kilometers pressing down on us.. The only reason we aren't crushed is our blood exerting an equal counteracting force. Interestingly, because air is a gas, a fluid, it exerts force not just downward, but also upward, sideways, and in every directioni maginable. Sounds impossible, right? Gravity should make sure air only applies force downwards. But think about a boat sailing on the sea, it only stays up because of a force exerted on it by the water, another fluid. Otherwise, think of submerging a ping pong ball or a balloon in a glass of water. It's pretty hard because some kind of force pushes it upwards. This is called buoyant force, or upthrust, and it occurs in all fluids to varying degrees. It is through the manipulation of this upthrust and air pressure that aeroplanes are able to fly.

Bernoulli, a famous Swiss mathematician, was the first to discover a relation between the pressure air exerts and the speed at which it is travelling. In essence, the slower air moves, the more force it exerts. So, if we can change the speed of air, we can create a difference in pressure; a difference that will support the plane's weight. So how is it done?

The secret lies in the shape of the wings. The special shape of the wings is called 'aerofoil'. Aerofoil is curved on the top and flat on the bottom. It looks a bit like a blue whale! What this achieves is a difference in air speed on either side. Because of a bit of complicated physics, called the continuity equation, the curvature of the upper wing results in the air moving faster over it. Since it has to travel further, it speeds up to reach its destination at the same time as the air below. As stated before, this means the air above the wing exerts less pressure, applying less force downward. On the other hand, the slow-moving air below the wing exerts a larger force upwards, resulting in the aeroplanes ability to remain in the air. It's surprising that air can create a large enough force to lift an aeroplane, opposing gravity itself. However, we must keep in mind that air pressure is no trivial matter. It easily has the force to crush metal. The only reason we don't feel this is because our body has adapted to it well.

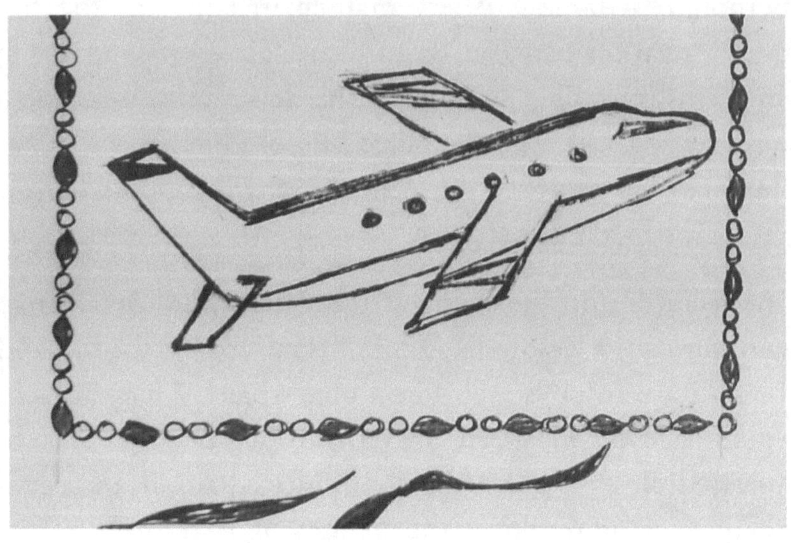

The Flying Bird

8

Why is it easier to swat a mosquito than a fly?

We've all been annoyed by a pesky mosquito that won't stop biting or a fly that won't leave our food alone.". You must have noticed that it's a lot easier to get rid of the mosquito than the fly, either by swatting it or using a mosquito repellent. Flies, on the other hand, dodge every attempt we make.

It turns out, flies are quite an agile species. The faster they are, the faster they can find food in the wild. More importantly, they have adapted this way to escape predators.

With their erratic flight patterns, it becomes much more difficult to figure out where they'll end up next. However, the key to their fast reaction time is their well- developed compound eyes. Compound eyes are structures seen in several insects and crustaceans, including mosquitoes. Unfortunately, the eyes of mosquitoes are not as adept at detecting rapid movements. Compound eyes consist of many smaller units called ommatidia. Each ommatidium has its own lens and light-sensitive cells, similar to our eyes. Because each ommatidia points in a slightly different direction, it allows the fly to see almost

360 degrees around it. Since there are so many sensory inputs, it gives the fly a crystal-clear image to detect any motion around it. Their superior compound eyes are one of the main reasons flies are so agile.

In addition to their superior eyesight, flies have extremely powerful wing muscles that beat hundreds of times per second.. They have a dedicated muscle system which adjusts the wing speed and direction of the wings, separately. Mosquitoes, on the other hand, have much weaker wings and a less efficient muscle system. Therefore, flies with their lightweight body, and exceptionally fast nervous system, dodge danger with ease.

Swatting a mosquito

9

How is a rainbow formed?

A rainbow is one of nature's most beautiful sights. Have you ever been driving and suddenly seen a gorgeous rainbow on the motorway, arching across the sky behind a signboard?" It's a sight to behold!

I am sure you have stopped to wonder, how such a pretty phenomenon comes to be. To understand how a rainbow forms, we need to know how light works. Light doesn't always travel in a straight line; it can bounce, change direction, or split into different colors. Only when it avoids a change in environment, does it travel in a straight line. So, when does it change direction? Well, you have heard of reflection, of course!

When a ray of light hits a certain surfaces, it bounces off at an equal angle.

However, light can also change direction in the air. When it passes from one medium, like air, to another, like water, it bends. It changes the angle at which it is travelling by a definite amount. This phenomenon is known as refraction.

his happens because light slows down when it travels through water." It resembles a car driving from a concrete road to a sand pit at an angle. Say the right wheel of the car reaches the sand pit first. The right wheel will slow down, while the left wheel moves at its normal pace. This causes the car to turn to the right. Eventually the left wheel reaches the sand pit, and both wheels now move at the same pace. This stops the car from turning further, and it now carries on straight with its direction changed from the original.

However, this still doesn't explain how rainbows are made. Where do all the colours come from? It turns out, white light is the combination of all colours of the spectrum, and the light the Sun emits is white. When you shine 7 rays of different colours, the result is a white, bright, and blinding light. You can try it out yourself! If you mix red, orange, yellow, green, blue, indigo, and violet paint, you will end up with white. So, it follows, if we are able to split white light, we should get these respective colours.

Now, how do we split light? Remember that light changes its angle during refraction? Well, different colours of light change their angles by different amounts. So, if we were to shine white light into a body of water, its constituent colours would be bent by different amounts, thereby separating them. This phenomenon is called dispersion. Finally, all the pieces are in place to make our rainbow. It all happens when a ray of light hits a water droplet (that's why you need it to be raining and Sunny at the same time). The ray splits into its constituent colours and is bounced around in the raindrop by reflection. When it emerges, we get a beautiful spectrum of colours. Several raindrops performing this phenomenon together lead to a rainbow.

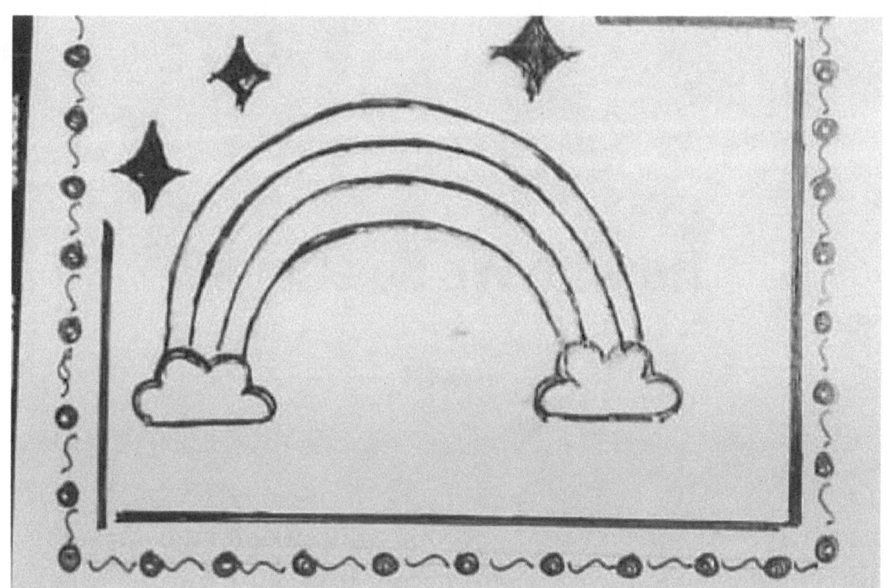

The Smiling Rainbow

10

How Do We See Color?

It's hard to imagine a world without color. Color adds meaning to everything we see, from art and nature to beauty. Yet the question arises: how do we perceive color? Why do things even have color?

Since we need light to see in the first place, it follows that light must have something to do with color. White light—the light we get from the Sun and lightbulbs—is composed of a spectrum of colors, from red to violet. Each of these colors is associated with a frequency, which you can think of as a measure of how energetic a particular ray is, with violet being the most energetic and red the least.

Every visible object has a natural affinity for certain frequencies of light, meaning it reflects some colors more than others. So, when white light falls upon an object, it absorbs certain frequencies and reflects others. The colors corresponding to the reflected frequencies are what we perceive as the object's color. For example, leaves appear green because they absorb all frequencies except green, which is reflected back to our eyes. In summary, objects appear to have a certain color because they reflect that color while absorbing others.

Now the question arises: how do we perceive this color? When a ray of light is reflected and reaches our eye, it enters through the pupil. The cornea and lens of the eye direct the ray to a point at the back of the eye called the retina. The retina contains sensory cells called photoreceptors, which are classified into rods and cones. Rods detect shades of gray and dim light but cannot detect color. Cones, on the other hand, are responsible for color perception. Humans have three types of cones: S-cones that detect blue light, M-cones that detect green light, and L-cones that detect red light. This combination of red, green, and blue light allows us to perceive a wide spectrum of colors.

For example, if you open any painting application, such as MS Paint, it allows you to choose the 'RGB value' of a color. This RGB value is simply the ratio of red to green to blue in the color you want to paint with.

Perception of Colours

But you might ask: how does a light ray hitting our eye get perceived as a color? It turns out that, depending on the input from the cones that pick up the rays, a nerve called the optic nerve sends an electrical signal to the brain. This electrical signal informs our brain of the color we are seeing, allowing us to understand the colors around us.

11

Why do we like some vegetables and hate others?

We know that vegetables are essential to a balanced diet. To maintain it, we need a sufficient intake of carbohydrates, proteins, healthy fats, vitamins, minerals, and roughage. Without these, we may encounter health complications down the line. Being mindful of what you eat and resisting temptation are key to staying fit and leading a healthy life.

But it really isn't that easy, is it? As a kid, I couldn't stand some vegetables. I wouldn't touch parwal, bitter gourd, or spinach. Something about them just threw me off. So why is it that some vegetables are so unappealing, while foods like pizza and burgers are so tempting?

It all comes down to two factors. The first is the evolution of human taste. We, as a species, have been hunter-gatherers for a long time. When Homo sapiens lived in caves, hunted for food, and stayed out in the scorching sun, energy was of utmost importance. Going days without food was common. To find food, we needed the energy from it—a cycle of nutrition. The most efficient sources of energy were carbohydrates, fats, and sugars. Protein was mainly useful for muscle repair. Remember, bodybuilding wasn't a thing back then! They were only chasing deer, not wrestling gorillas! Although vitamins and minerals are essential for preventing disease, they don't provide many calories. So, our taste buds slowly developed a preference for carbohydrates and sugars. Most of us have a sweet tooth as a result, and who can say no to a fatty, cheesy pizza? Unfortunately, vegetables were deprioritized, despite their immense nutritional benefits.

The Taste of Vegetables

The other factor, also a result of evolution, is the bitterness of many vegetables. Unlike fruits, which are meant to be eaten by animals to spread seeds, vegetables are part of the plant itself. To prevent animals from eating these parts, plants evolved to secrete bitter chemicals. These compounds include glucosinolates (found in broccoli, cabbage, and sprouts), alkaloids (found in tomatoes and potatoes), and tannins (found in spinach and other leafy greens). In nature, most bitter substances are toxic, deterring herbivores from nibbling on defenseless plants.

However, this is not an excuse to stop eating your vegetables! These evolutionary traits are remnants of the past. Modern science shows that vegetables are crucial for a healthy life.

Besides, you might eventually come to enjoy them. It happened to me—now I can't go three days without parwal in my meals. So, give them a chance!

12

What's the most important invention?

Inventions, inventions galore! They are a testament to human creativity and have led us to where we are today. Surprisingly, some of the greatest and most useful inventions were accidental, discovered in attempts to create something else. For example, tea bags were originally just a way to send leaf samples to customers. The X-ray was discovered by a scientist experimenting with the newly developed Crookes tube (a device used to visualize electrons), and zippers were first invented for boots. These examples show that invention is the perfect blend of luck, genius, and creativity.

Unfortunately, it's difficult to pinpoint the single most important invention. There are so many that have influenced our history, and if we were to remove even one, our reality would be vastly different. However, I won't leave you empty-handed! We all know the popular inventions credited as the cradles of civilization: fire, the wheel, electricity, the internet, and penicillin. So, why don't I share a few unexpected ones?

First, let's talk about anesthesia. Anesthesia, a chemical inhaled or injected to numb the body, transformed medicine. Before the discovery of the first anesthetic, surgery was a painful and life-threatening ordeal. Often, to spare patients terrible pain, surgeons would rush their operations, sometimes making fatal mistakes. Interestingly, the first anesthetic discovered was laughing gas. However, its effects were too short-lived, leading to a search for alternatives. Soon, an ether-based anesthetic was developed, followed by chloroform, which proved to be long-lasting. These anesthetics were so successful that one mother even named her child "Anaesthesia!"

Next, let's consider the printing press. Books hold knowledge, and knowledge is the key to human progress. What happens, though, when sharing information relies solely on writing books by hand? Progress becomes sluggish. Therefore, when Johannes Gutenberg invented the printing press in 1440, he became a catalyst for scientific advancement. Now people around the world could share ideas with minimal effort. The printing press enabled the mass production of books by setting text in a metal cast, covering it in ink, and pressing the cast onto paper. Without it, many of the inventions that followed might not have been possible.

Finally, there's the barcode—the arrangement of lines you see on library books and grocery items. Invented by Norman Woodland and Bernard Silver in the 1950s, a barcode is simply a series of numbers and lines that a machine can read. Yet it led to a revolution in management and efficiency. By assigning a unique code to each item in a warehouse, grocery store, or library, inventory management became computerized. No longer would an employee need to manually log every item in and out. Instead, each item could be scanned, instantly updating its status in the system.

This simple invention has saved an immense amount of manpower, time, and money.

The inventions that revolutiuonised

13

How do windmills work?

With the increasing demand for clean energy, many countries have turned to windmills. Places like the Netherlands are famous for their vast landscapes dotted with these towering machines, all working together to provide energy. Isn't it a sight to behold? But how do these ever-spinning pillars work?

Let's start with a bit of history. Windmills date back to the 7th century, where they were used in ancient Persia and China. They were rudimentary structures made of reeds and wood, primarily used to crush grain into flour or pump water for irrigation. The blades, or sails, of the windmill were connected to a shaft. When the sails caught the wind, they rotated along with the shaft. To grind grain, a pair of millstones (large stone slabs) was used: the upper stone was connected to the shaft, while the lower one remained fixed. Grains placed between the stones were crushed into flour as the upper stone rotated.

To pump water, the windmill was engineered a bit differently. Here, the shaft was connected to a crank system (a piston linked to a wheel). As the wheel turned, it enabled an up-and- down motion, which pumped water from a well.

In the 19th century, with the onset of the Industrial Revolution, the need for windmills declined. The invention of the steam engine brought new sources of power, and factories soon began burning fossil fuels. Over time, windmills became a thing of the past.

Today, however, the demand for clean energy has brought windmills back. They are a green source of electricity that minimizes environmental impact. Now, the wind turns the shaft, which in turn rotates a generator, supplying electricity to nearby neighborhoods.

The turning windmills

14

Why can we erase pencil but not pen?

I remember the day in class 6 when I was finally allowed to use a pen. My teachers had deemed me skilled enough to write in ink without making mistakes. Until then, we were restricted to using pencils only. Any mistake we made could be erased, and though our work might not have looked perfect, it was free from cross-outs. But have you ever wondered, "Why is it so easy to erase pencil but not ink?" When we try to erase ink, it just smudges and spreads; it doesn't vanish like pencil marks.

To understand why, let's look at the structure of each. Pencils use a mixture of clay and graphite (a carbon compound) encased in wood. When you write with a pencil, graphite particles are deposited onto the paper and stick due to intermolecular forces—forces between the paper and pencil molecules. Since these particles only sit on the surface of the paper and don't penetrate it, they can be easily removed. The eraser, made of rubber, creates friction to loosen the paper's grip on the particles, and its slightly sticky surface picks up the graphite.

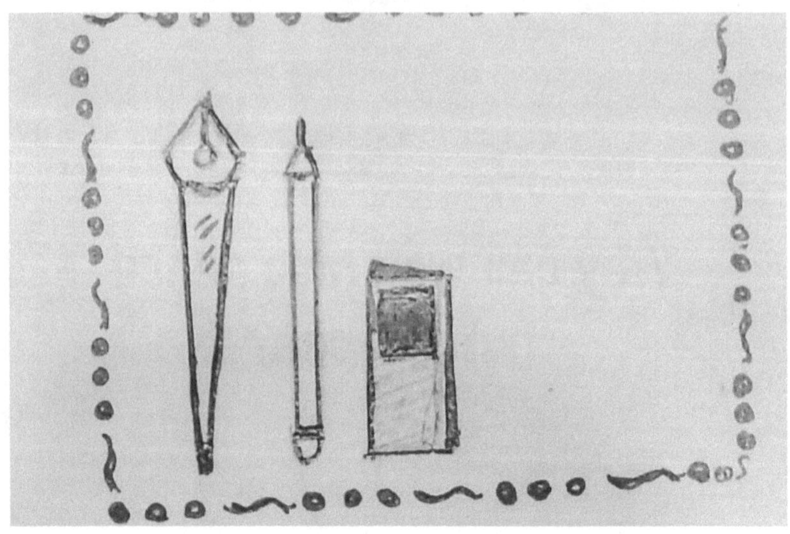

The trio of pen-pencil -eraser

This process, however, doesn't work for ink. Pens use liquid ink, which is either water-, oil-, or gel-based. When you write with a pen, the ink soaks into the paper fibers rather than resting on the surface. Oil and gel-based inks even form chemical bonds with the paper, making them much harder to smudge or remove. As a result, erasing ink "stains" from paper is nearly impossible.

Some pens now feature erasable ink. These aren't your typical pens; they use a special ink that neither penetrates the paper deeply nor chemically bonds with it.

15

Why do we build dams?

Every other day, a dam makes headlines. These colossal, man-made structures—often a hundred times taller than the average human—aren't built just for fun! Dams like the Hoover Dam are celebrated as pinnacles of architecture, so there must be something extraordinary about them!

Dams reflect the importance of rivers throughout human history. Dating back to the Mesopotamian and Indus civilizations, dams were initially constructed to control water resources for irrigation and drinking. When a dam is built across a river, it halts the flow, causing the river to overflow and form a large water body called a reservoir behind the dam. The water from this reservoir can be used for drinking or redirected through channels. A flowing river is prone to seasonal flooding and droughts, making it unpredictable. By creating a dam, neighboring land gains a steady, year-round water source, allowing for safe irrigation channels that won't drown crops during floods.

Today, dams are often used to generate electricity. They are typically built over rivers that descend from great heights, much like a waterfall. The flow through the dam is controlled by gates that can be opened or closed as needed. Water released through the gates falls onto a turbine generator, turning its blades and moving a magnet inside to generate electricity.

The flowing Dam

16

How do submarines work?

Submarines are our gateway to a hidden world. Thanks to them, we can explore stunning marine flora, fascinating fauna, and uncover the secrets of the ocean. Submarines have been pivotal to deep-sea exploration and are incredible machines. But submerging and resurfacing a vehicle of that size isn't simple. So, what's the science behind it? Submarines rely on the principle of buoyancy.

Have you ever gone swimming with a kickboard? When you try to push it underwater, you'll feel a strong upward force pushing it back. This force is buoyancy, and submarines use it to dive and surface.

Where does this force come from? Fluids exert pressure in all directions. For any submerged object, there is always an inward pressure. This pressure increases with depth, which is why deep divers must wear protective suits to withstand the water pressure.

The interesting thing about this pressure is that it's always greater beneath an object than above it, creating a net upward force on the object. Imagine a die with side 1 on top and side 6 at the bottom, submerged in water. Sides 2, 3, 4, and 5 are at the same depth, so they experience equal pressure. But since side 6 is deeper than side 1, the pressure on side 6 is higher, creating an upward force. Archimedes discovered that this upward force (the buoyant force) is proportional to the volume of the object. Larger objects experience more buoyancy, so a large, light object floats, while a small, heavy one sinks.

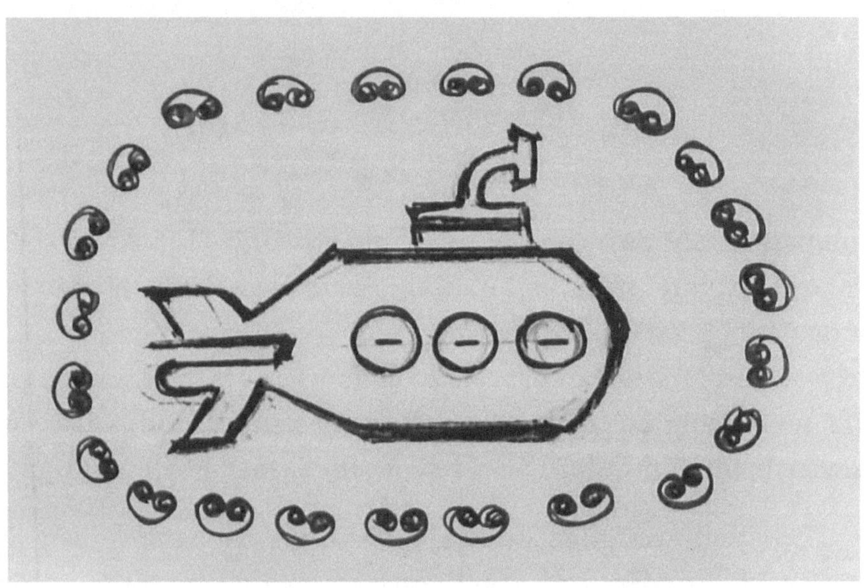

The Underwater Submarine

So, how does a submarine use this force? Submarines are equipped with ballast tanks—large compartments that can hold air or water. The volume of the submarine remains the same, but its contents and weight can change. When the submarine wants to dive, it fills the ballast tanks with water, making it heavier than its buoyant force, causing it to sink. The rate of descent is controlled by how much water enters the tanks. To maneuver along the ocean floor, it uses propulsion engines and propellers. When it's ready to resurface, it expels water from the ballast tanks and fills them with air. Since air is lighter than water, the submarine becomes lighter than the buoyant force and rises to the surface.

It's important to remember that the buoyant force is constant and always tries to push the submarine upward. By adjusting the weight, we control whether the submarine sinks or resurfaces.

17

How does a generator work?

I'm sure we've all experienced this situation. It's a dark, stormy night. Rain pours down relentlessly outside. You're sitting comfortably in your room, safe from the chaos, when suddenly, the lights go out. The fan stops spinning, and you're left in total darkness. Your mother calls for the generator to be switched on, and soon, everything comes back to life.

The word "generator" seems self-explanatory, yet there's a mystery to it. From its name, it clearly generates electricity—but how? Let's dive into it.

When we talk about electricity in our homes, we're referring to the electric current supplied to us through power lines and wires. Electric current is simply the movement, or flow, of electric charge carried by electrons. To get this current flowing, we need a push, called electromotive force or voltage, which drives the charges along a wire. The stronger this force, the faster the charges move, and the higher the current. A generator's role is to produce this electromotive force, thus restarting the current in our household wires.

But how does the generator create this force? Let's go back to 1831 when Michael Faraday discovered electromagnetic induction. He found that moving a magnet around a wire would produce an electric current. The physics behind it involves terms like magnetic flux and the rate of change of flux. In simple terms, changing a magnetic field's strength or direction can generate a force that pushes charges along a wire. This discovery paved the way for widespread electricity generation.

To power an entire neighborhood, we need a large magnet, rapid movement, and numerous coils of wire, so generators in power stations operate on a much larger scale. The generator in your home, however, operates on the same basic principle. When it detects a power cut, it begins burning fuel (usually diesel or petrol) to power a motor, moving the magnet through the coil. This movement generates the electromotive force needed to supply electricity to your home.

The Dependable Generator

18

How does a violin work?

The violin has been an integral part of classical and orchestral music since the 16th century. You'll rarely find a symphony without it, and the number of influential violin sonatas is countless. Many of the movies and TV shows we watch rely on violins to set their themes and moods. Truly, it is a masterpiece of craftsmanship. But how does an instrument like this create such beautiful melodies? Each instrument has unique mechanics; let's delve into those of the violin.

The violin consists of a wooden frame with four strings stretched along it. It is played by drawing a bow—horsehair tied to a wooden holder—across the strings. The horsehair can be tightened for better sound quality, and before playing, rosin is often applied to the bow to enhance its grip on the strings.

To produce sound, the bow is drawn across the strings, causing them to vibrate. Friction between the bow and strings initiates the vibration, and the pitch of the sound produced depends on the tightness, length, and mass of each string. The four strings provide a wide range of frequencies, but violinists can modify pitch further by pressing down on a string at different points, shortening the vibrating portion. This allows a violin to produce frequencies from around 196 Hz to 3520 Hz.

The Sounds of the String

But what gives these vibrating strings their rich, resonant sound? Plucking a rubber band might produce a note, but it doesn't sound like Vivaldi's *Four Seasons*! In the violin, the sound is amplified by its wooden frame. A small, arched piece called the bridge holds the strings taut and transmits their vibrations to the body. Inside, a rod known as the "sound post" carries these vibrations through the instrument.

The amplification comes from resonance. Resonance occurs when sound waves of the same pitch interact, intensifying the sound. Vibrations from the bridge and sound post cause the air inside the violin to vibrate at the same frequency. These vibrations reinforce each other, creating a fuller, more resonant sound. The specific shape and size of the violin body further enhance this resonance, like a Helmholtz resonator, to produce the vibrant and powerful sound that has captivated listeners for centuries.

19

How does a piano work?

The piano is the figurehead of music. With its vast range of notes and capacity to play intricate chords, complex rhythms, and serenading melodies, it has cemented its place in the musical world. You'll rarely encounter a composition that doesn't include it, as it's an essential tool and a powerful force in music. But its sound doesn't come from thin air—so where does it originate?

Inside a piano lies a hidden system of hammers, strings, and resonators working in harmony to produce each note. Each of the 88 keys is connected to a lever mechanism called the "action." When a key is pressed, this action lifts a hammer, which then falls to strike a string within the piano. If you've ever peeked inside a grand piano, you've likely seen these strings.

Each string also has a damper. When the key is released, the damper comes down, stopping the string's vibration and thus ending the note.

The strings are precisely crafted with specific lengths, tensions, and masses to produce their respective notes. For many notes, particularly those in the middle to high pitch range, the piano uses unison strings—two or more strings struck simultaneously—to create a fuller sound. High-pitched notes, in particular, are softer by nature since their strings are thin, light, and less efficient at transferring energy. Unison strings boost their volume, creating a more resonant tone.

Like all instruments, the piano relies on resonance to produce a rich, powerful sound. Resonance is a phenomenon where sounds of the same pitch amplify one another, resulting in a louder, more vibrant sound. In a piano, this resonance occurs when vibrations from the strings transfer to the soundboard, a large, flat piece of spruce. The soundboard amplifies and projects the sound into the air. The way sound waves reflect and interact within this space contributes to the piano's characteristic depth and resonance.

The Tapping Keys

20

How does a guitar work?

The guitar stands as an icon of the music industry. Its versatility has cemented its role in genres like rock, blues, jazz, and classical, with the power to shape both modern and traditional music around the world. From its ability to create melody and harmony through chords and riffs, it's a staple in countless songs and musical styles. But what makes the guitar truly remarkable lies in its simple yet effective design, rooted in centuries-old traditions.

The guitar's history can be traced back to ancient Mesopotamia and Egypt, where early stringed instruments like the tanbur and oud were played. These instruments had long necks and rounded, hollow bodies. Over time, other instruments with similar designs, such as the lute, vihuela, and baroque guitar, became popular in Europe. Despite differences in shape and structure, all these early guitars had one common feature: a hollow, rounded interior. This feature, although seemingly subtle, is key to the guitar's ability to produce rich, resonant sound.

When a guitarist plucks a string, the string vibrates at its natural frequency, which depends on its length, tension, and mass. To adjust the pitch, the guitarist presses down on the string, shortening the vibrating length and increasing its frequency. These vibrations travel through the bridge—a small wooden piece—into the soundboard and, finally, into the hollow body of the guitar, which acts as a resonating chamber. Resonance is a phenomenon in which sounds of the same frequency amplify each other, creating a louder, fuller tone. Within the guitar's hollow body, sound waves bounce and blend, resonating together to produce a rich and resonant note.

Electric guitars, on the other hand, rely on a different mechanism. Instead of a resonating chamber, they use magnetic pickups that detect string vibrations and convert them into electrical signals. These signals can then be amplified electronically, giving the electric guitar its unique, powerful sound.

This combination of centuries-old acoustic design and modern technology has solidified the guitar's place in music across the world. Let me know if you'd like further adjustments or more details!

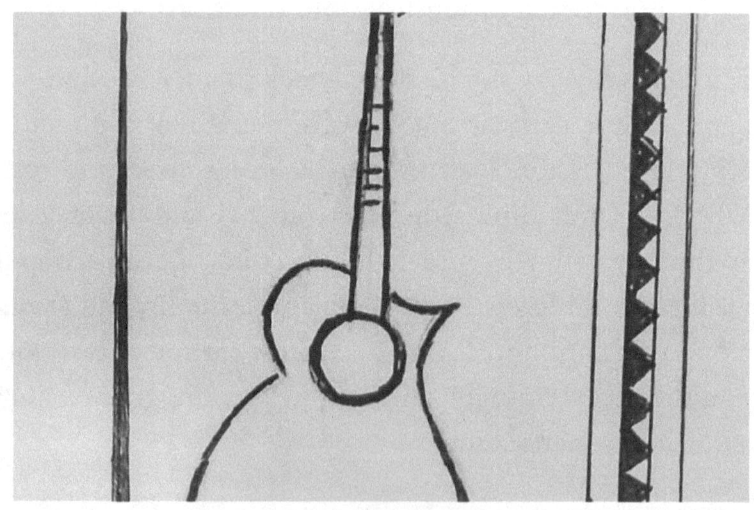

Strings and sound signals

21

How does a drum work?

Drums have been a part of human life since prehistoric times, setting the rhythm for our ancestors and influencing music, culture, and society. Early humans made the first drums from hollow logs or bones, covering them with animal skins to create a tool that could signal across distances or scare off wild animals. As civilizations like Mesopotamia, Egypt, China, and African cultures emerged, drums took on an even deeper role. They became integral to religious and ceremonial practices. Around 2,000 years ago in ancient India, the "mridangam" became highly popular, serving in rituals, armies, and recreation. Over time, this legacy culminated in the modern drum kit in the 20th century, influenced by jazz and rock music, which combined traditional drums with cymbals.

But what is it about a drum's structure that gives it its iconic sound? The secret lies in the design of the drumhead, a taut membrane stretched across the drum shell. When struck, the energy from the drumstick causes the drumhead to vibrate, setting off rapid vibrations that transfer into the air within the drum shell. This creates waves that bounce back and forth inside the shell, blending with the vibrations resonating along the shell's walls.

This interaction of waves generates resonance, a phenomenon where sound waves of the same pitch merge and amplify, creating the powerful, booming sound of the drum. The open end of the drum, or sound hole, allows these amplified sound waves to escape, creating the distinctive beat that we hear. Adjusting the tension of the drumhead also changes the pitch— tighter for a higher sound, looser for a deeper tone—allowing the drum to create various rhythms.

From ancient rhythms to modern music, drums remain an enduring and powerful presence, keeping humanity's beat alive.

The Drum Beats

22

Why is ice slippery?

Slips and falls

Ice's slippery nature is something we encounter all the time, from struggling to hold an ice cube to witnessing an ice skater glide across the rink. Unfortunately, this slipperiness can also lead to hazards, as cars often skid on ice-covered roads, causing accidents. But why exactly is ice so slippery?

It all comes down to melting points and pressure. Normally, a solid turns to liquid when heat is applied, breaking down the strong intermolecular forces that hold its molecules tightly together. This process occurs at a specific temperature known as the melting point, when the molecules gain enough energy to vibrate freely and break these bonds. For most solids, applying pressure raises the melting point, as pressure restricts the expansion needed during melting.

However, ice is different from most solids because of water's unique property: it actually contracts when melting rather than expanding. So, applying pressure to ice actually nudges it towards its liquid state, lowering its melting point. When you hold an ice cube, for instance, the warmth from your hand and the pressure you exert combine to melt the outer layer, creating a thin film of water that makes it slippery.

For ice skaters and vehicles on icy roads, this phenomenon plays a significant role. The thin blades of an ice skate, coupled with the skater's weight, generate enough pressure to create a slick film of water on the ice surface. Similarly, a car's weight exerts enough pressure on the ice to form a water layer, causing it to lose traction. The result is a smooth, frictionless surface that allows gliding or, unfortunately, a loss of control.

In this way, ice's slippery nature is a fascinating example of how unique physical properties—like pressure-induced melting—transform solid surfaces into slick, watery layers.

23

Why is water wet?

Water - the eternal life source

Water is essential to life, and we encounter it in countless ways every day. From drinking to cleaning, bathing to cooling, water is always close at hand. But why does water have such unique and familiar qualities—why does it make things wet, feel cool to touch, and seem slippery? Let's explore each of these properties to uncover the science behind them.

When we say something is "wet," we're describing how water alters an object's physical feel and weight. Firstly, water has a cooling effect on anything it touches due to its high specific heat capacity. This means it absorbs a lot of heat without its temperature rising much. For instance, to heat just one liter of water by 1°C requires as much energy as a smartphone uses in 20 minutes! Because water absorbs heat so well, it feels cool to touch and is used in cooling systems worldwide, from car radiators to nuclear reactors.

Next, water makes objects feel heavier when they're soaked. This is especially obvious with cloth or fabric. Water seeps into all the tiny spaces within the fibers of a material, filling them up and adding weight. A liter of water weighs a kilogram, so even a small amount of water absorbed by fabric significantly increases its weight.

Finally, there's the matter of slipperiness. Water acts as a lubricant, reducing friction between surfaces. Typically, friction resists movement, allowing us to grip objects. However, water molecules have weak intermolecular forces, meaning they easily slip over each other. This low friction coefficient makes wet surfaces feel slick. Water also has strong adhesion properties, which means it clings to surfaces readily. When we touch a wet surface, water sticks to our fingers, but the layers of water between our fingers and the surface can easily slide over each other, creating that slippery sensation.

In summary, water's high heat capacity keeps it cool to touch, its density makes soaked objects feel heavier, and its low friction and strong adhesion make it slippery. Together, these properties explain why water acts the way it does and why it's so effective in shaping our world.

24

How do microphones and speakers work?

Speakers and microphones are cornerstones of modern technology, allowing us to communicate and experience music, movies, and more. Though they seem different, they are actually complementary devices: speakers turn electrical signals into sound, while microphones convert sound into electrical signals. Let's break down how they work.

To start, sound itself is a wave. When you speak, air molecules vibrate in a pattern of compressions (high density) and rarefactions (low density), creating a longitudinal wave that our ears detect. A simple example of this is the childhood cup-and-string telephone: if you pull the string taut between two cups, sound waves from one cup vibrate the string, which then transmits these vibrations to the other cup, where they turn back into sound waves.

Microphones take a similar approach, but they do it with electricity. Inside a microphone, there is a thin membrane called a diaphragm. When sound waves hit this diaphragm, it vibrates at the same frequency as the sound. There are two common microphone designs:**Dynamic Microphones:** Here, the diaphragm is connected to a small coil of wire. As the diaphragm vibrates, the coil moves within a magnetic field, generating an electric current. The variations in current match the vibrations, creating a signal that mirrors the original sound.**Condenser Microphones:** In this type, the diaphragm is one of two closely spaced metal plates (a capacitor). As the diaphragm vibrates, it changes the distance between the plates, altering the capacitance. This creates an electric signal corresponding to the sound waves.

Speakers essentially reverse this process. The speaker receives an electric current from a device like a computer or phone, where the strength and frequency of the current reflect the sound's pitch and volume. Here's how it works:

1. **The Electric Current and Coil:** The current flows through a coil of wire inside the speaker. This coil sits in a fixed magnetic field, and because of inductance, it generates its own magnetic field that mirrors the current.

2. **Magnetic Interaction:** The coil's magnetic field interacts with the surrounding field, creating a push-pull effect that moves the coil back and forth.

3. **The Diaphragm and Sound Wave:** As the coil moves, it pushes and pulls on a diaphragm attached to it. These movements create compressions and rarefactions in the air, forming sound waves that we hear as music, voices, or other audio.

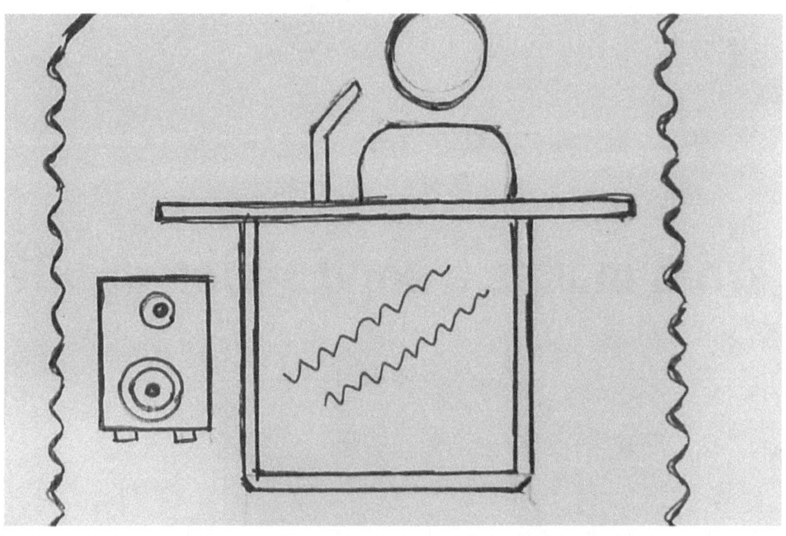

The duo of microphone and speaker

In essence, microphones detect sound by converting air vibrations into electrical signals, while speakers generate sound by turning electrical signals into air vibrations. This complementary pairing enables much of our technology, from phones and video calls to concerts and cinema.

25

What makes a song sound good?

Music is an integral part of human culture, weaving itself into our lives as a means of expression, communication, and entertainment. Its ability to unify communities and convey emotions makes it a powerful force. From various styles and genres to the unique structures of songs, music reflects and shapes human experiences, connecting us with others and providing a way to articulate our deepest feelings. While the forms of music may evolve, its fundamental role as a vehicle for expression and cultural identity remains constant. But what makes music so enjoyable?

Dopamine and Pleasure: Listening to music triggers the release of dopamine in the brain, a neurotransmitter associated with pleasure and reward. When we anticipate our favorite songs or hear a captivating chord progression, dopamine levels surge, leading to feelings of euphoria. This biochemical reaction explains why music often elicits joy and enhances our mood.

Emotional Regulation: Music also influences our emotional state through the brain's limbic system, which regulates feelings. Research shows that music can lower cortisol levels, the hormone associated with stress, while increasing oxytocin, which promotes relaxation and bonding. This capacity to evoke emotional responses is a key reason why music resonates with us.

Pattern Recognition: Our brains are wired to recognize patterns, a trait that has been crucial for our survival and development. This innate ability extends to music; each song features an array of melodies and rhythms. When the brain anticipates a chord progression, it experiences satisfaction. Conversely, unexpected rhythms bring pleasure, reinforcing our enjoyment. This relationship between music and pattern recognition highlights why music is so compelling to our brains.

Lyrics and Connection: Lyrics in songs often resonate more deeply than prose. When meaningful messages are delivered through music, they strike a personal chord, leaving a lasting impact. Songs that reflect our struggles or celebrate our joys create a profound connection, making us feel understood and less alone. Our brains seem to favor storytelling in musical form, as it allows us to engage with narratives on a more emotional level.

Music for our ears

In summary, the enjoyment of music stems from a complex interplay of biochemical responses, emotional regulation, cognitive pattern recognition, and personal connection. It enriches our lives, enhances our well-being, and serves as a vital part of our shared human experience.

26

What would happen if the Sun disappeared?

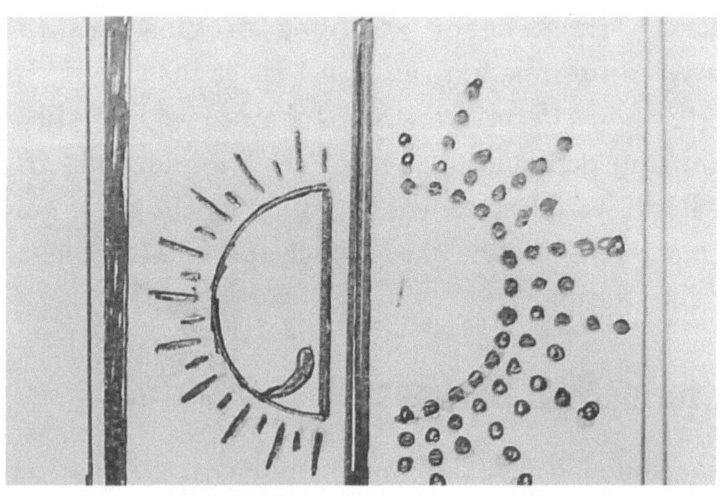

Life without the sun

The idea of the Sun disappearing is indeed a chilling thought! The Sun is crucial for life on Earth, providing the light and energy necessary for all living things. If such a catastrophic event were to occur, the immediate consequences would be fascinating yet terrifying.

The Initial Reaction

Imagine you're going about your day, blissfully unaware of the cosmic upheaval. As you walk down the street, the Sun suddenly vanishes. For the next **8 minutes and 20 seconds**, everything seems normal. This time frame is significant because it takes light approximately **8 minutes and 20 seconds** to travel from the Sun to Earth. During this period, you wouldn't notice any changes in brightness or warmth because the light from the Sun would still be reaching us.

The Gravity of the Situation

A common concern is whether we would feel the effects of gravity immediately. Interestingly, according to **Einstein's theory of relativity**, no information can travel faster than light. Therefore, the gravitational effects of the Sun's absence wouldn't be felt until that same time period elapsed. Once the 8 minutes and 20 seconds are up, Earth would no longer be bound by the Sun's gravity and would move in a straight line through space, much like an object thrown into the air.

The Aftermath of Darkness

After the initial delay, darkness would envelop the Earth. The immediate aftermath would see a dramatic drop in temperature. While Earth might retain some warmth from its internal energy, this would not last long. Within a week, average surface temperatures could plummet to around **-73°C** (-100°F).

The Frozen Landscape

The cold would cause Earth's surface to freeze. However, the oceans could provide a glimmer of hope. A layer of ice would form on top, acting as an insulator and retaining heat beneath the surface. Many deep-sea organisms rely on geothermal energy and would continue to thrive, demonstrating nature's resilience in the face of such adversity.

Human Survival

For humans, the situation would be dire. Without the Sun, agriculture would fail, leading to food shortages. We would face extreme challenges to our survival. However, ingenuity might prevail. Through the use of **artificial heating and light**, it could be possible to create habitable environments, at least in the short term.

While the thought of a sunless world is unsettling, it serves as a reminder of how interconnected life on Earth is with our star. The Sun's disappearance would bring about a cascade of effects, dramatically altering life as we know it. Thankfully, this is purely theoretical, and our Sun remains a steadfast source of light and energy in our solar system.

27

How do we get sick?

Falling ill is never fun. Often, we are left bedridden and feverish, with the sole benefit of not having to go to school. Our breath becomes hot and shallow, our body aches all over, and the

pain feels unbearable. Sometimes, our stomach hurts, or hives erupt across our skin. Although illness is a natural part of life, it is unpleasant to deal with. So why does it happen?

Illness is caused by pathogens—a term for harmful microorganisms like bacteria, viruses, parasites, and fungi. Illness can also result from our body reacting to allergens and toxins.

When we get sick, our symptoms are a result of pathogens harming various parts of the body and our immune system fighting back. The immune system responds by releasing white blood cells to attack these invaders, leading to inflammation, redness, heat, and swelling in the skin. To create an unfavorable environment for pathogens, our body raises its temperature, which results in a fever but helps kill germs. In rare cases, the immune system mistakenly attacks the body's own cells, leading to autoimmune diseases. Though our immune system may be inefficient at times, it is actively trying to protect us. The symptoms are often a good sign, proving that our body is fighting back.

However, symptoms caused by pathogens manifest differently depending on the type of pathogen and its location. For example, bacteria that multiply and release harmful toxins in our body may cause a urinary tract infection (a painful infection of the urethra) or a sore throat.

Sad to be sick

Viruses, on the other hand, insert themselves into cells and take them over. The virus then forces the cell to replicate more viruses. To prevent a complete takeover, our body raises its temperature and increases mucus production, leading to fevers and colds.

Fungal infections occur when yeast or mold grows on the body's surface, damaging the skin and causing visible changes.

Finally, parasites, like tapeworms or the malaria-causing *Plasmodium*, feed on the body's nutrients, resulting in general weakness and other disease-specific symptoms.

It is important to note that most serious diseases can be prevented. By washing our hands and practicing good hygiene, we can eliminate many germs that aim to invade our bodies. So remember to take care and maintain basic hygiene practices

28

What if everyone jumped at the same time?

It's fun to fantasize about improbable events. After all, how would we even get all the people in the world to jump simultaneously? But let's imagine it happened. What would follow?

Unfortunately, not much. The sight would certainly be a spectacle, but it wouldn't cause any visible changes to the Earth's surface.

Using the population density of New York as a reference, the entire human population could fit comfortably within the borders of Turkey. If we gathered everyone for a massive jump and had them stand shoulder-to-shoulder, they'd only cover an area the size of the city of London. So, let's assume this scenario. We manage to convince everyone to gather in London and jump together on the count of three. What happens next is anticlimactic: the Earth would shift by a mere 1/100th the diameter of a hydrogen atom. This is because Earth weighs approximately 6,000 yottagrams, or 6×10^{24} kg, and the force required to move it even a centimeter is unimaginable.

Together jumping high

On the "bright" side, the combined jump would generate an energy equivalent of about 5,000 tons of TNT. However, this still isn't enough energy to cause an earthquake or shift the Earth's tectonic plates. When everyone lands, there might be minor tremors, but these would be no more intense than those caused by a large sporting event. There would hardly be any damage to the concrete beneath. Though the force of the jump would be significant, it would be spread across such a large area that the stress exerted on the ground would be minimal.

Thus, we reach an unsatisfying conclusion to a fascinating question.

29

How does A.I work?

Artificial Intelligence, or A.I., is a fast-growing field with enormous, untapped potential. A.I. refers to the simulation of human intelligence through machinery and electrical signals, aiming to emulate cognitive functions like learning, reasoning, problem-solving, and pattern recognition.

But it might seem impossible to simulate human intelligence through a series of 1s and 0s (binary code), doesn't it? Let's look at how it's done.

To imitate humans, A.I. must first understand us. It gathers large amounts of data from even the smallest actions, observing various inputs and their corresponding "correct" outputs. For example, A.I. might receive images of the sky, a pair of jeans, the ocean, and a blueberry (inputs) and learn that these objects are blue (the output). The machine recognizes patterns from these examples and gradually learns what the color blue entails. This pattern recognition relies on neural networks and deep learning. Neural networks are designed to mimic the human brain and its neural connections. Each network is made up of nodes (like neurons) that process information. Deep learning advances this concept by layering multiple neural networks for a more sophisticated analysis.

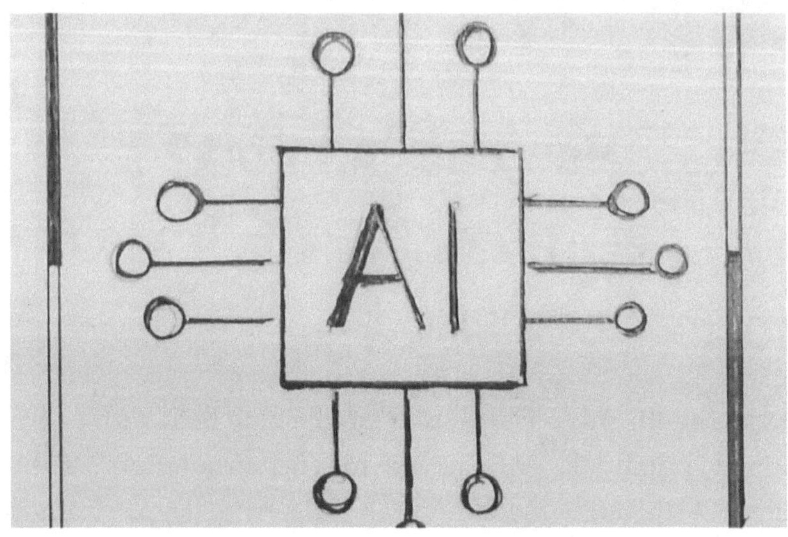

Our future in AI

To understand language, A.I. uses Natural Language Processing (NLP), which enables it to mimic human speech and language through techniques like tokenization, parsing, and sentiment analysis. NLP powers chatbots like ChatGPT and voice assistants like Siri and Alexa, allowing A.I. to respond to questions in a human-like manner.

Through reinforcement learning, A.I. can improve and evolve independently. The model receives rewards or penalties based on its interactions—similar to Pavlov's dog. This feedback loop enhances its performance over time.

It's important to note that A.I. models can be biased. If they are trained on biased or limited data, they may produce faulty results.

30

What is the fastest thing in the universe and why can't we go faster?

All roads have speed limits. Under no circumstances should one be driving a car at 120 km/h on a city road. These restrictions are mandatory and unwavering. If you exceed the speed limit, the consequences are severe. So, is it the same for the universe? Is there a universal speed limit?

It turns out there is—the speed of light! The speed of light is 2.99×10^8 m/s, an incredibly large number. For context, the fastest human-made object, the Parker Solar Probe, travels at 191 km/s, which is only 0.064% of the speed of light. Yet, the universe is so vast that it still takes light centuries to travel across a galaxy.

But why can't light, or anything else, go faster than this? We owe this "speed limit" to James Maxwell and Albert Einstein. Maxwell proved that the speed of light is constant, regardless of the reference frame. For example, when we travel in a car, we see trees on the highway moving backward. We know they are stationary, but because we're moving forward, they appear to move backward—this is known as relative motion. It's also why a car traveling alongside us appears stationary, even though it's moving. However, Maxwell showed that light does not obey relative motion: everyone sees light moving at the same speed, regardless of how fast they are moving.

For instance, a stationary person sees light traveling at 2.99×10^8 m/s. A person in a car moving at 60 km/h also sees light traveling at 2.99×10^8 m/s. Even if someone were moving near the speed of light itself (say, 2.98×10^8 m/s), they would still see light moving at 2.99×10^8 m/s, not stationary. This property of light indeed warps time and space.

Albert Einstein refined this idea through his Special Theory of Relativity. He argued that as an object moves faster, its mass effectively increases. The closer it gets to the speed of light, the more massive it becomes, requiring exponentially more energy to continue accelerating. Through a complex set of calculations, Einstein showed that if an object approached the speed of light, it would gain infinite mass, thus requiring infinite energy. Einstein also demonstrated that as speed increases, time slows down for the moving observer. This fascinating yet complex concept implies that if you were to travel at the speed of light, time would stop altogether—everything around you would seem to happen at once.

Fastest First

31

How do screens display images?

Electronic devices have become an integral part of our lives, required in almost everything we do. Most of these devices are equipped with a display. Devices such as computers, mobile phones, billboard signs, and TVs rely heavily on displays. Let's take a closer look at how these displays work.

A display screen is made up of countless pixels. The higher the number of pixels, the better the resolution and clarity of the images displayed. Modern computer screens, for example, have over 2 million pixels! Pixels, short for "picture elements," are small boxes that emit light in various colors. To achieve a full color spectrum, an RGB scheme is typically used. Each pixel is divided into three sub-pixels—red, green, and blue. By adjusting the brightness of each sub-pixel, a pixel can display any desired color. For example, when red and blue are at full brightness and green is off, the pixel appears pink. An image, therefore, is simply a combination of differently colored pixels.

But how does a pixel emit light in the first place? Several technologies make this possible, including LCD, OLED, and CRT.

The mechanisms of display

LCD, or Liquid Crystal Display, screens contain liquid crystals sandwiched between two glass plates. The crystals themselves do not emit light but instead modulate the intensity of RGB light. Light in LCDs comes from an LED (light-emitting diode) positioned behind the pixels. The LED provides the necessary illumination for the display.

OLED stands for Organic Light Emitting Diode. In these displays, each pixel is made of organic compounds that light up when electricity passes through them. OLEDs allow for flexible screens that can be bent and shaped.

CRT, or Cathode Ray Tube, technology involves firing electrons at the screen's surface. This surface is coated with materials that emit light when struck by electrons.

32

How do we know what time it exactly is?

Time is a funny thing. Everything seems to follow it. We wake up at 7 a.m., eat lunch at 1:30 p.m., and go to sleep around midnight. Offices open at 9 a.m., and schools start by 8. The world runs on punctuality, and to be punctual, we need to know the time. But how do we know the exact date and time?

No one handed humans a universal clock; we created timekeeping ourselves. The ancient Egyptians are credited with the first calendar, realizing its importance in planning the irrigation of their crops. Every 365 days, the Nile would flood, watering crops and bringing nutrient-rich silt. The Egyptians needed a way to track these 365-day cycles to plant their seeds accordingly. They observed the length of days based on the Sun's position and noted the appearance of the star Sirius, which signaled the Nile's flooding. This led to their creation of a calendar year. They divided the year into 12 months—11 with 30 days each and a 12th with 35 days. Each month had three weeks of 10 days. They also divided the year into three seasons: Akhet (flooding or inundation), Peret (crop-growing), and Shemu (harvest).

Later on, the ancient Sumerians created their calendar by observing the cycles of the Moon. Each month corresponded to the time it took for the Moon to go from a new moon to a full moon and back again. The Mayans created an exceptionally accurate calendar that closely matched the actual length of a year. The Babylonians, Chinese, and Romans further refined the calendar. Finally, the Gregorian Calendar, introduced by Pope Gregory XIII, became the most widely used. It bases its year zero on the birth of Jesus Christ and divides the year into the 12 months we know today.

For timekeeping, we again have the Egyptians and Mesopotamians to thank. Knowing the Sun rises in the east and sets in the west, ancient societies observed the Sun's consistent, apparent movement across the sky due to the Earth's steady rotation. This allowed them to divide the day into 12 equal segments based on the Sun's position. They used sundials to track these segments: a simple rod perpendicular to a plate marked with 12 lines around its perimeter. As the Sun moved, the rod's shadow cast on the plate moved, indicating the time.

Modern clocks were developed much later, with the most precise being pendulum clocks, invented in 1656 by Christiaan Huygens. These clocks measure seconds based on the swing of a pendulum—a small mass attached to a long rod or string. Once set in motion, a one- meter-long pendulum will take approximately one second to swing from one side to the other, nearly regardless of its release height. Each swing of the pendulum advances a gear inside the clock, moving the second hand slightly. Once the second gear completes a full rotation, the minute gear moves the minute hand, which, in turn, moves the hour hand.

For a long time, pendulum clocks were the primary method of keeping time until they were replaced by quartz clocks, which count seconds using the vibration of a quartz crystal. These are the battery-powered wristwatches many of us use today. These watches are calibrated according to the standards set by the International Bureau of Weights and Measures (BIPM) and the National Physical Laboratory (NPL), responsible for standardizing and tracking time worldwide.

The turning time

33

How does probability work?

Probability is a fascinating concept. In practice, it seems simple, but its effectiveness and scope are remarkable. Probability helps us make informed decisions in finance, explain phenomena in quantum physics, assess the risk of medical procedures, and even forecast weather. By calculating the likelihood of an event, probability allows us to quantify the risk of one option over another. It is essential in fields like statistics, economics, science, engineering, and even daily decision-making. We often use a basic form of probability in our daily choices, making decisions based on previous experiences.

Let's see how it works.

At its core, probability tells us how likely an event is to occur. The probability of a chosen event is calculated by dividing the number of ways that event can occur by the total number of possible outcomes. For example, the probability of rolling a 2 on a die is 1 (since only one side of the dic shows 2) out of 6 (since a die has six sides). The probability of rolling an odd number is 3 out of 6, since there are three odd numbers (1, 3, and 5). It's important to remember, however, that probability is not a guarantee. If we roll a die six times, there's no certainty that a 2 will come up even once; it's also possible to roll a 2 six times in a row.

Probability simply tells us how likely an outcome is, not that it will definitely happen.

Sometimes, we need to calculate the probability of two events happening together. In simpler cases, the outcomes of these events don't affect each other. Some events are "mutually exclusive," meaning they cannot happen simultaneously. For example, if we pick one ball from a bag of colored balls, we cannot pick up both a blue and a red ball at the same time. To calculate the probability of mutually exclusive events, we add their probabilities. So, if there are 10 red, 10 blue, 10 green, and 10 yellow balls in a bag, the probability of drawing either a red or a blue ball is 10/40 + 10/40 = 1/2.

Some events are "independent," meaning they can happen at the same time, but the outcome of one doesn't affect the other. For example, if we toss a coin in one hand and roll a die in the other, the probability of getting heads and a 2 on the die are independent events. The probability is therefore 1/2 (probability of heads) × 1/6 (probability of rolling a 2) = 1/12. If we were to list all possible outcomes (1 and heads, 1 and tails, etc.), we would find there are 12 possible cases, confirming that our formula aligns with the definition of probability.

Mutually inclusive events, where the outcome of one affects the probability of the other, are interesting but more complex. Solving such problems requires conditional and Bayesian probability, which goes beyond the scope of this book.

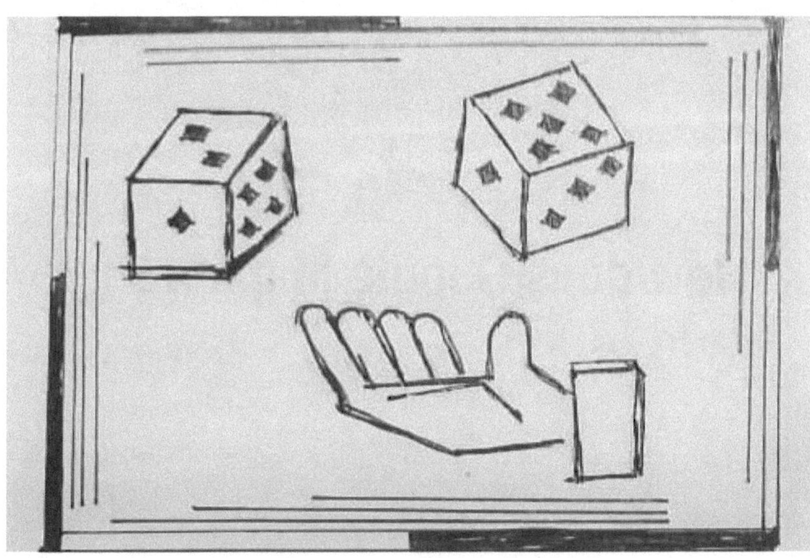

How probable is probability

34

How does Google Maps work?

Our modern road guide

Imagine a hiker with a passion for climbing. One day, he sets off to conquer an infamous trail through a scenic mountain pass. For days, he treks onward, setting up camp where he can.

Each morning, he breathes in the sweet-scented air and feasts his eyes on sprawling landscapes. He couldn't ask for a better expedition. But then, disaster strikes—a thick fog rolls in, obscuring the trail. Now unsure of his location and direction, he remembers his mobile phone. Luckily, there's a signal nearby. He quickly opens Google Maps, which tracks his position and guides him safely to the nearest shelter.

Technology like this can be lifesaving. But how does it work? How does it know exactly where we are and which way to go?

Google Maps is a web-based service that provides map-based navigation, real-time traffic information, and location details. It's the culmination of groundbreaking technologies like GPS (Global Positioning System), Wi-Fi, cell towers, and data mapping. Google Maps relies on multiple sources to provide its services. To determine exact location, it uses a GPS receiver, which communicates with several satellites. Each satellite sends a signal to the receiver, containing the satellite's position and the precise time the signal was sent. Since the satellites are in different locations, their signals reach the receiver at slightly different times.

The receiver calculates the time taken for each signal, multiplies it by the signal speed, and finds the distance to each satellite. By measuring distances to three separate satellites, Google Maps can triangulate the user's location.

When GPS is weak, such as in dense urban environments or indoors, Google Maps uses Wi- Fi signals and cell towers to help pinpoint location, using a similar triangulation method.

To build detailed maps, Google uses Street View cars that regularly drive around capturing panoramic images of streets worldwide. Google Maps also licenses map data from governments, municipalities, and commercial providers to ensure accuracy.

To find the optimal route, Google Maps calculates multiple options, considering distance, real-time traffic conditions, and other factors. It tracks traffic by analyzing the speed at which its users are traveling. If vehicles slow to a crawl in a certain area, Google Maps detects congestion and stops recommending that route to other users.

Recently, Google Maps has begun using AI and machine learning to predict traffic patterns, estimate travel times, and offer better route suggestions. Through this intricate process, Google Maps is able to guide us efficiently to our destinations.

35

Why do we sleep?

After a tiring day of work or school, there's nothing more appealing than a good night's rest. Stretching out on a soft, comfy bed is one of life's greatest pleasures. But it begs the question: why do we sleep?

Sleep is an essential bodily function with numerous biological and psychological benefits. Although much about sleep remains a mystery, we do understand some key aspects. The human body undergoes constant wear and tear throughout the day, from physical activity to merely existing. At night, during sleep, the body repairs tissues, builds muscle, and strengthens the immune system. Growth hormones like somatotropin are secreted to aid in this recovery.

Another essential benefit of sleep is energy conservation. While awake, the brain and body consume a large amount of energy, demonstrated by a higher metabolic rate. When we're asleep, this rate drops, and the body's energy demand decreases. This helps us replenish and store energy, preparing us for the next day.

Sleep also plays a crucial role in cognitive functioning and memory consolidation. Throughout the day, our brains process massive amounts of information, some of it useful and some of it not. During sleep, the brain strengthens the important neural connections and discards unnecessary ones. This enhances critical thinking, creativity, and decision-making,

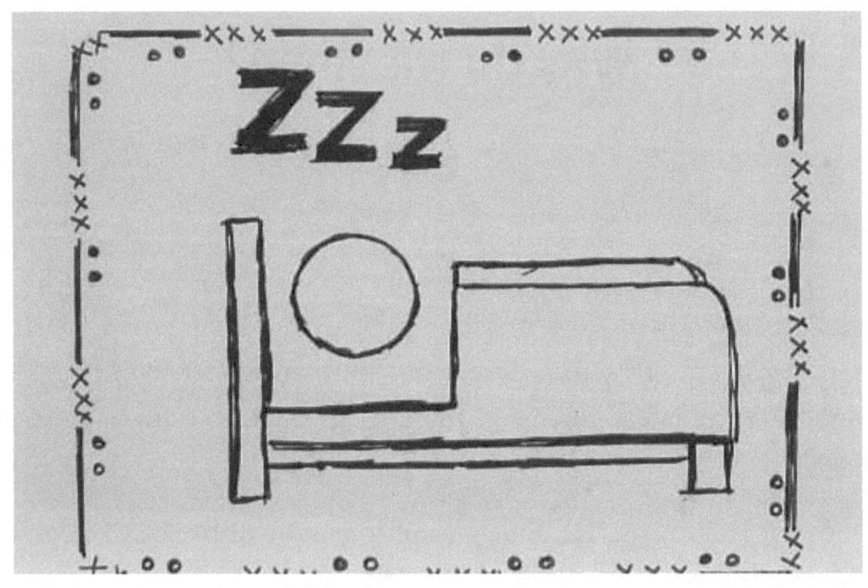

Is this your favourite past-time

while also helping us retain information by moving memories from short-term to long-term storage.

Emotionally, sleep is vital for stability. While asleep, the amygdala—the brain's emotional regulation center—rebalances. Naturally, poor sleep can lead to irritability, stress, and, in severe cases, depression and anxiety.

Sleep also has significant physiological effects. The immune system releases cytokine proteins during sleep, which fight infections and inflammation. Sleep aids in clearing waste products from the brain, including harmful proteins like beta-amyloid, which has been linked to Alzheimer's. It also regulates hormones involved in hunger, metabolism, and appetite, like ghrelin and leptin. Finally, sleep is crucial for heart health. As we sleep, blood pressure drops, allowing the heart and blood vessels to rest. Chronic sleep deprivation, on the other hand, has been associated with heart disease, stroke, and high blood pressure.

36

How does soap keep us clean?

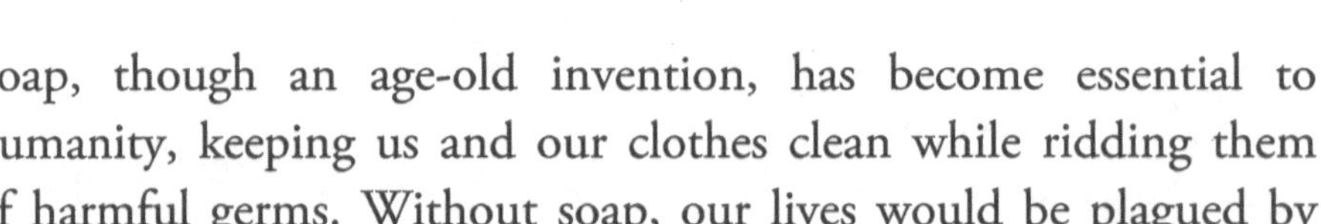

Soap, though an age-old invention, has become essential to humanity, keeping us and our clothes clean while ridding them of harmful germs. Without soap, our lives would be plagued by diseases and pests. While the Middle Ages saw much suffering due to poor hygiene, today soap plays a crucial role in our daily lives, protecting us from harm. But how exactly does it work?

To understand how soap works, let's first explore how it's made. Soap is produced from fats or oils combined with an alkali through a process called saponification. This process breaks down fats into fatty acids and glycerin, which then interact with the alkali. Fats can come from animal sources, like tallow or lard, or from plants, like olive oil or palm oil. Sodium hydroxide is used for solid soaps, while potassium hydroxide is used for liquid soaps. This difference occurs because the smaller sodium atoms form tightly bound molecules with fatty acids, creating a more solid structure. Potassium atoms are larger and form looser bonds, resulting in a softer, more soluble soap. Saponification produces glycerol as a byproduct, which can be left in the soap to add moisture or removed for cosmetic reasons.

The resulting soap molecules consist of two parts: a hydrophilic (water-attracting) head and a hydrophobic (water-repelling) tail. This means that the soap molecule has an end that attracts water molecules and an end that repels them. The hydrophilic head is derived from the alkali and fatty acid reaction, forming a salt, while the hydrophobic tail comes from the remainder of the fatty acid structure. When we apply soap and water to our skin, the hydrophilic heads of the soap molecules attach to the water, with the hydrophobic tails pointing away. These tails latch onto oils and dirt, forming structures called micelles around each dirt particle. The micelles are then suspended in water, allowing the dirt to be rinsed away.

Soap also disrupts the fatty membranes of bacteria and viruses, effectively deactivating them. This combination of effects is what enables soap to keep us clean and protect us from dirt and germs.

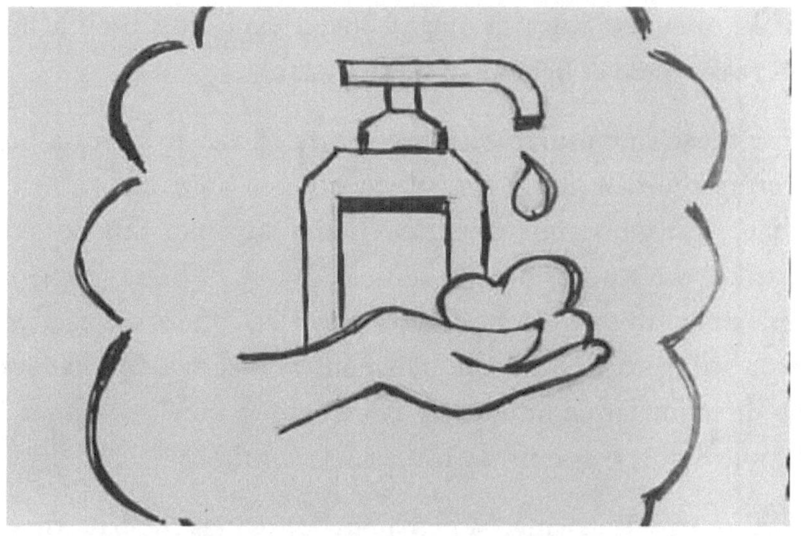

Soapy hands, squeaky clean

37

How does a cricket ball spin?

Sports are an essential part of life, offering both fitness and enjoyment. For me, cricket has always held a special place. I remember spending evenings in the local park, playing with my father and brother. My brother would often pick up the bat, while my father and I took turns bowling to him. Spin-bowling has always intrigued me; I was naturally inclined towards it and loved exploring how a bowler could make the ball behave so unpredictably.

For those unfamiliar with the sport, cricket involves a bowler delivering the ball along a pitch to bounce once before reaching the batsman, who aims to hit it. If the batsman misses and the ball strikes the stumps behind him, he is out. While cricket has its complexities, this is the basic idea. Bowlers often use tactics like spin or swing to deceive the batsman. Spin bowling changes the ball's direction after bouncing, while swing bowling causes it to drift mid-flight. But how do these tricks work?

Let's start with swing. When a bowler swings the ball, they give it a rotation. This creates a physical phenomenon called the Magnus effect, which is based on Bernoulli's principle.

Bernoulli's principle tells us that in a moving fluid (like air), the sum of kinetic energy (related to speed) and pressure remains constant. If kinetic energy decreases, pressure must increase, and vice versa.

How does this relate to a swinging ball? As the ball spins through the air, it creates uneven airflow on each side. One side of the ball, spinning in the direction of the airflow, speeds up the air around it. The other side, spinning against the airflow, slows down the air. Think of it as one side "going with the flow" and the other "resisting." This uneven air speed causes a pressure imbalance: lower pressure on the side with faster-moving air and higher pressure on the slower side. The ball is "pushed" towards the side with lower pressure, creating the swing.

The art of spinning the ball

Now, onto spin bowling. Here, the bowler imparts a spin using their fingers or wrist, causing the ball to rotate on its axis. When the spinning ball hits the ground, it wants to "recoil" and reverse its spin direction—much like how a bouncing ball returns upward after hitting the ground. This change in spin direction is due to friction between the ball and the pitch. The bowler's skill lies in spinning the ball so that this friction not only alters the spin but also changes the ball's direction.

This is why pitch conditions are so crucial for spin bowling; if the pitch lacks enough grip or friction, the ball won't spin as effectively.

38

Why does the Earth spin?

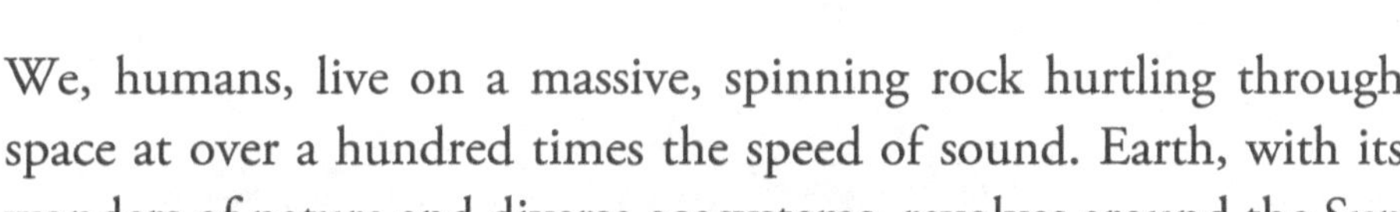

We, humans, live on a massive, spinning rock hurtling through space at over a hundred times the speed of sound. Earth, with its wonders of nature and diverse ecosystems, revolves around the Sun and spins on its axis, giving us the warmth, days, and nights that sustain life. But why does Earth continue to spin and orbit the Sun?

Let's start with Earth's orbit around the Sun. The Sun is a massive star, with enough mass to exert a significant gravitational force. Newton's theories of gravity tell us that objects with large masses have strong gravitational pulls. While Earth's gravity is strong enough to keep us grounded, the Sun's gravitational pull is even more substantial. So, why doesn't Earth just fall into the Sun? This is where inertia comes in.

Inertia is the tendency of an object in motion to keep moving in a straight line unless acted upon by another force. If there were no gravitational pull from the Sun, Earth would travel in a straight line across space. However, the Sun's gravity continuously pulls Earth toward it.

The balance between Earth's inertia, which keeps it moving forward, and the Sun's gravitational pull, which draws it inward, results in Earth's circular orbit. In a way, Earth is constantly "falling" towards the Sun but also moving forward quickly enough to avoid crashing into it. Gravity and inertia are in a continuous dance, keeping Earth in orbit.

The spin which matters

Now, why does Earth spin on its axis? For this, we need to go back about 4.5 billion years to the formation of our solar system. Back then, the solar system was a massive cloud of gas and dust known as the solar nebula. Under the force of gravity, this material began to clump together, forming the planets. As each new planet took shape, it inherited a rotation from the swirling material that formed it. This rotation was set in motion and, due to Newton's first law (an object in motion stays in motion), Earth kept spinning.

Since space is a vacuum, there's nothing to slow this spin—no ground friction, air resistance, or fluid to cause drag. Thus, Earth continues its spin, just as it has for billions of years.

39

How does the metro train work?

Metro railways, or underground trains, are a vital part of urban transportation, forming a bustling network beneath our feet. They offer a fast, reliable, and eco-friendly mode of transit, reducing car reliance and supporting workers who commute long distances.

Establishing a robust metro system is crucial to a city's growth and functionality. So, how do governments go about setting one up?

Metro systems operate through a combination of electric power, control systems, and solid engineering. Most are powered by electricity, delivered either through an overhead wire called a catenary or a third rail. Electric motors propel the train, with traction motors on the wheels or axles driving its movement. Power and speed are managed by either a train operator or an automated system. Automatic Train Operation (ATO) controls speed, acceleration, and braking, while Automatic Train Protection (ATP) prevents the train from exceeding safe limits. This symbiotic control ensures metro trains run smoothly, arrive on time, and stop precisely at platforms. Trains use regenerative braking, where the electric motors function as generators to recover some energy during braking, enhancing efficiency.

To maintain safe distances and coordinate movement across the network, trains rely on advanced communication and signaling systems. These systems regulate train spacing and route coordination, while the trains themselves run on standard-gauge rails with specialized steel wheels designed for smooth, efficient travel.

Designing metro routes is a meticulous process, combining urban planning, engineering, and economic analysis. High-density areas are identified as key nodes, and existing road and bus networks are studied to find areas where a metro could reduce congestion. Routes connect residential zones, commercial hubs, and major landmarks, with stations positioned in high- demand areas. Once planning is complete, construction begins.

Detailed surveys assess soil and rock conditions to determine the tunnel's depth, diameter, and excavation method. One popular approach is using a Tunnel Boring Machine (TBM), where large, rotating cutters break through rock and install pre-cast concrete to line and stabilize the tunnel. Where TBMs are less effective, controlled explosives are sometimes used.

In the Cut-and-Cover method, a trench is excavated from the surface. A concrete or steel tunnel is constructed within the trench, which is then backfilled upon completion. Lastly, the Sequential Excavation Method involves digging small sections of the tunnel at a time, stabilizing each section immediately before moving forward. After excavation, a permanent lining is installed, laying the groundwork for the intricate transit ecosystem below our feet.

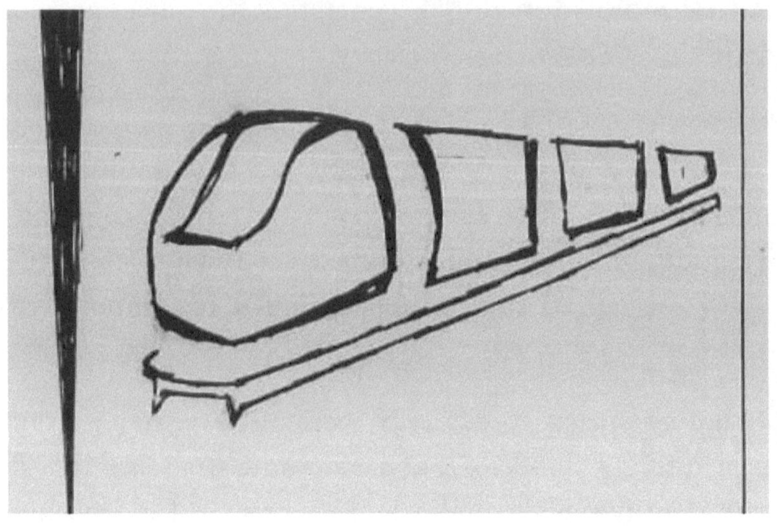

The metro connecting cities

40

Why do clothes dry faster when kept outside?

When I was younger, I'd spend hours playing outside in the scorching sun with friends. We'd run around, kicking a football until dusk. Then came the rain, offering relief from the heat. The sheer joy of being drenched was invigorating as we leapt and danced in the downpour, hardly noticing our exhaustion. When the rain finally stopped, we'd head home, shivering from head to toe. My mother would scold me to change clothes, and she'd hang my soaked garments outside. By the next day, they'd be crisp and fresh, as if by magic. But of course, it was science at work!

The drying process is simply the removal of water, which has seeped through the tiny pores in the fabric. Since ancient times, we've used the sun to dry clothes by evaporating the water – transforming it from liquid to gas. This is similar to boiling, but evaporation isn't quite the same. Boiling happens at a specific temperature—100 degrees Celsius for water—while evaporation occurs at much lower temperatures. Importantly, evaporation is a surface phenomenon, whereas boiling is a bulk process. In boiling, all the water converts to steam, while with evaporation, only surface molecules gradually turn to gas.

Both processes, though, stem from the same reason: molecules breaking free as they gain enough kinetic energy. In solids, molecular bonds are strongest, while in liquids, they're weaker but still present. In gases, they're barely detectable. When a water molecule overcomes the force of attraction, it escapes into a gaseous state. In boiling, we apply heat directly, energizing all the molecules and causing them to break free together. Evaporation, however, is more gradual. Surface molecules of liquids, like water, are loosely bound and easily carried away by even small amounts of energy.

So, why does evaporation happen faster outdoors? Four key factors are at play: First, sunlight speeds up the process, as its warmth energizes molecules to break loose. Second, sunlight acts as a natural disinfectant, killing microorganisms that might bind water molecules to the fabric. Third, air circulation hastens evaporation; moving air carries away molecules from the surface, especially when there's a strong breeze. Finally, humidity matters: on a dry day, with low humidity, the air can absorb more moisture from the clothes. If the air is already saturated with water vapor, it can't hold much more.

Dry them fast

These straightforward physical processes allow our clothes to dry easily, thanks to the sun, air, and the natural power of evaporation.

41

How does a fan work?

The ceiling fan has become essential in hot, sweltering climates. Without it, high temperatures would be nearly unbearable. Fans provide a simple, efficient way to cool our homes, but how do they accomplish this?

A ceiling fan consists of a set of blades that rotate rapidly due to a motor inside. This motor, powered by electricity, generates rotation through the interaction between magnets and electric currents. By positioning a coiled wire within a magnetic field, a torque is created, causing the coil (and any connected blades) to spin. Increasing the current in the coil or strengthening the magnets can further boost the speed of rotation.

With the mechanical aspects understood, let's explore why ceiling fans actually cool us down. The cooling effect of fans relies on facilitating evaporation, working in sync with our body's natural cooling process. When we sweat, our bodies are attempting to cool down by allowing sweat to evaporate. This phase change—where liquid sweat becomes vapor—requires energy. This energy is absorbed from the heat of our skin, lowering our body temperature.

As higher-energy molecules leave, the remaining molecules have lower energy, reducing the overall temperature.

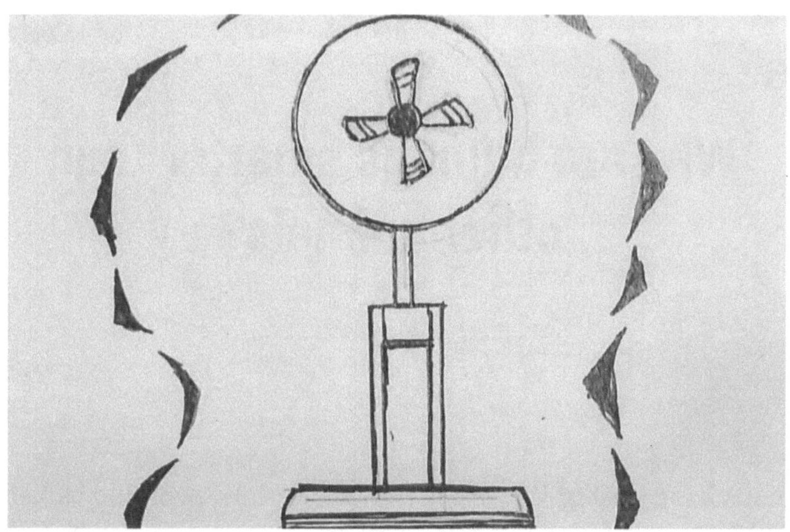

The essential friend on a hot day

Ceiling fans speed up this process by circulating air evenly throughout the room. The gentle breeze they create replaces the humid air around us with drier air, which can absorb more moisture. When air becomes too saturated with water vapor, it can't hold much more, and the evaporation rate decreases. By constantly refreshing the air, fans keep the rate of evaporation steady, enhancing the cooling effect and helping us feel more comfortable

42

Why are humans smarter than other animals?

Humans have existed for nearly 3 million years, evolving as a species to take on new challenges and overcome obstacles. Discoveries such as fire, the invention of the wheel, and the rise of civilization are testaments to our intelligence. We are creative and conscious beings, but what sets us apart from the animals around us? Why do we possess an understanding that they do not?

The primary difference lies in the structure and function of our brains. Humans have a highly developed neocortex, the brain region responsible for reasoning, problem-solving, and abstract thinking. This area allows us to process complex information, predict outcomes, and plan for the future. Although humans have fewer overall neurons than larger creatures like elephants and whales, we have a greater density of neurons in the neocortex. Larger animals often need their neurons to manage their size and bodily functions. In contrast, humans have a high brain-to-body ratio, enabling us to support more neural connections that enhance our cognitive abilities without expending energy on locomotion.

Furthermore, humans have developed sophisticated language systems capable of expressing our desires and needs. This ability allows us to communicate abstract ideas and pass down knowledge through generations. The invention of tools has also transformed labor into ingenuity, giving us more time to explore other pursuits. Tools became gateways to creation and innovation, allowing us to form large societies where ideas and beliefs could intermingle. As we shared information and learned from our mistakes, we accumulated knowledge over time. Our self-awareness and capacity for metacognition—the ability to think about our own thoughts—enable us to analyze our ideas, mistakes, and problems. This unique ability to imagine things that do not exist and express those concepts fuels our boundless creativity.

But how did we acquire these remarkable gifts? Several theories attempt to explain why humans have evolved to such an extent, with the most intriguing being the "cooking hypothesis," proposed by Richard Wrangham. This hypothesis posits that cooking—particularly boiling carbohydrates—played a crucial role in human advancement. By cooking food, we made it easier to digest, allowing us to absorb more calories and nutrients. Cooking breaks down complex molecules, enhancing our digestive efficiency. The increased caloric yield from cooked food fuels the brain, which consumes about 20% of the body's energy.

Over time, human digestive systems evolved to become more compact and efficient, further freeing up energy for brain function.

The social implications of cooking also cannot be understated. Cooking fostered development and community. Around a roaring fire, men and women would converse, prepare meals, eat, and bond. While many factors contributed to the progress of humanity, the cooking hypothesis remains one of the most widely accepted explanations for our unique evolutionary path.

The Ultimate Genius

43

Why can birds fly but we can't?

Wouldn't it be wonderful if we could fly? Oh, to soar above the clouds! To roam freely over the Earth would be a dream come true. We could travel wherever we wished, visit undiscovered places, and take in breathtaking sights. But alas! We are grounded, with our feet firmly planted on the ground. No matter how hard one tries to flap their arms, they will never take off. So, why is it so easy for birds?

Birds can fly thanks to a remarkable combination of anatomical, physiological, and biomechanical adaptations. Through evolution, they have learned to overcome the forces of gravity and propel themselves through the skies. Their most striking feature is, of course, their wings. These wings have an airfoil shape—flat on the bottom and rounded on the top. Because of this shape, air moves faster over the top and slower underneath. According to Bernoulli's Principle, this difference in airspeed creates a difference in pressure. The resulting pressure difference generates an upward force known as lift, allowing the bird to rise into the air.

Birds also generate additional lift by flapping their wings. By forcing air downward, they create an equal and opposite reaction force that propels them upward. Their feathers are lightweight yet strong and are arranged on the wings to control airflow. This large surface area allows birds to generate the necessary force to take flight.

The freedom of flying

Moreover, birds have lightweight skeletons that enable them to reduce their overall weight without compromising strength. Their bones are fused in the pelvis and shoulders, providing stability and support, which is essential for flight. To produce the force required for flapping, birds are equipped with strong pectoral muscles in their chests, enabling them to flap harder and faster. They manipulate their tail feathers to steer, brake, and maintain balance, while their smooth, streamlined bodies and feathers minimize air resistance.

It's evident that humans are ill-equipped for flight. We do not possess the evolutionary features that birds have. In comparison to a bird's wings, human arms are too short and narrow for our body proportions. Our arms lack the necessary volume and airfoil shape required for flight. Furthermore, we do not have the proportional muscle strength needed; even the strongest bodybuilder would struggle to lift themselves off the ground. While birds may be weaker than us in absolute terms, they have a much higher muscle-to-bodyweight ratio, which is critical for flight.

Ultimately, we lack the hollow skeletons, the energy efficiency, and the specialized structures that birds have developed over millions of years. For now, we remain constrained to flying in planes and helicopters.

44

How does sound travel?

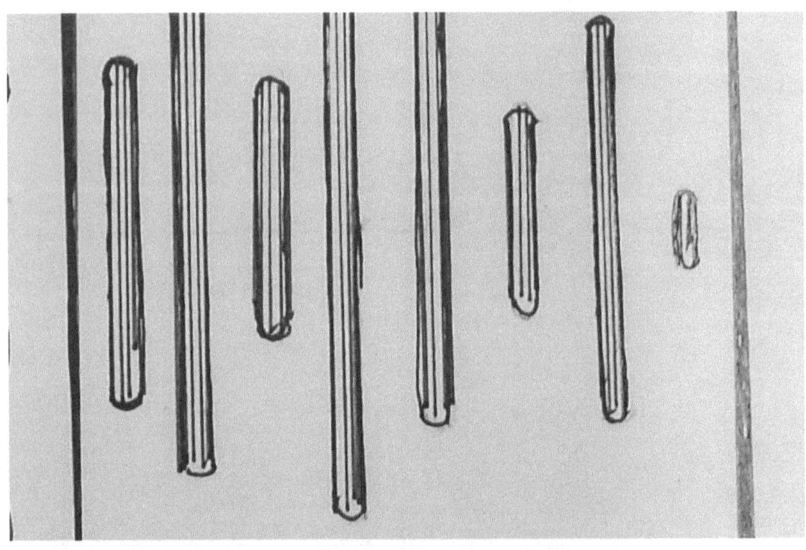

Sound travels - thus we hear

Sound is a mysterious phenomenon. We can shout from a mile away and still hear each other, yet if we whisper right up close, it may be barely audible. Sound can be shrill or flat, loud or soft, noisy or pleasant. But where do these properties come from? How does sound travel from one point to another? Why does sound appear clear above ground yet seem indistinct underwater?

It turns out that sound is a wave—similar to the ripples on a pond's surface. Sound requires a medium to travel through, whether it's air, water, or wood. In the emptiness of space, all sound is inaudible. A violently exploding star would not be heard even a meter away from it. This is not because the sound is too muffled, but rather because sound itself cannot exist in a vacuum. Let's explore why.

As mentioned earlier, sound is a wave created by the vibration of particles in the medium it travels through. This oscillation of particles transfers energy across the medium, enabling sound to propagate. Sound is produced by vibrating objects, such as a guitar string or our vocal cords. For example, the "thud" sound made by a falling box results from the vibration of the box and the floor, reverberating from the impact. These vibrations initiate a chain reaction, causing the surrounding air (or respective medium) particles to vibrate in turn. The strength and speed of the source dictate the loudness and frequency of the sound.

In most cases, sound travels as a longitudinal wave. In this type of wave, particles of the medium move back and forth along the direction of the sound. This can be likened to shaking a slinky (a spring-like toy). Shaking creates alternating regions where the coils bunch up together and regions where they spread out. These regions interchange, with the bunched-up areas spreading apart and the spread-out areas compressing together. This back-and-forth motion is analogous to sound waves traveling through air and other fluids.

Because of this property, sound travels fastest in solids and slowest in gases, with liquids falling in between. In gases, particles are far apart and move around freely, while in solids, particles are compact and closely packed. Thus, it is easier for the wave to reach the next particles in a solid, allowing sound to travel faster. Consequently, the denser a medium is, the faster sound travels through it. This is why sound is often clearer on a humid day—more moisture in the air increases density.

Now that we understand how sound moves, let's explore how we perceive it. Our ears are adept at picking up the vibrations of air. The eardrum vibrates in response to these sound waves, which then move through a chain of tiny bones in the ear. The auditory nerve detects these vibrations and converts them into signals that the brain can understand.

Interestingly, one might expect that we should hear better underwater, given that sound travels faster and clearer through water. However, the human ear is adapted to pick up vibrations through air. Any sound we perceive underwater is actually sensed through the vibrations of our tissues and skull! There is a pocket of air present in our ear, and when sound in water encounters it, it is forced to compress.

45

What did Einstein do to make him so famous?

We all know the name Albert Einstein—one of the smartest individuals to have ever walked the Earth. It's common to jokingly refer to geniuses as "Einstein." As a renowned physicist, he is credited with some of the most significant scientific advancements in history. While many of us are familiar with terms like "$E=mc^2$" and "relativity," they can often feel like

buzzwords, their meanings lost in abstraction. Let's delve into Einstein's work to uncover what he truly accomplished.

Einstein is credited with several groundbreaking developments in physics, but his magnum opus emerged in 1905, a year often referred to as Einstein's "Annus Mirabilis" or "Miracle Year." During this time, he published four pivotal papers in the scientific journal *Annalen der Physik*, which significantly contributed to quantum mechanics, our understanding of light, the theory of relativity, and Brownian motion. Let's explore each of these papers.

In March 1905, Einstein published a paper on the photoelectric effect—a term that may sound complex but describes a straightforward concept. When light shines on a material (usually a metal plate), it ejects electrons (tiny subatomic particles responsible for electricity). The number of ejected electrons can be measured by the electric current they produce.

Einstein observed that the number of electrons ejected was not dependent on the brightness of the light but rather on its frequency, meaning that increasing brightness alone would not increase the number of photons. This finding was contrary to classical physics, which stated that the energy of light should depend on its intensity rather than its frequency. Einstein resolved this puzzle by building on Max Planck's quantum theory, proposing that light possesses both wave and particle characteristics—known as wave-particle duality. Although this concept can be challenging to visualize, the mathematics supports it, forming the foundation of quantum physics. Einstein explained that light consists of packets of energy called photons, with energy proportional to the light's frequency. When a photon strikes a material, it transfers some or all of its energy, ejecting an electron in the process. This breakthrough not only laid the groundwork for quantum physics but also facilitated advancements such as solar panels and light sensors. For this work, Einstein received the Nobel Prize in Physics in 1921.

In May 1905, Einstein published a paper on Brownian motion, providing a theoretical explanation for the erratic motion of particles suspended in a fluid. This explanation played a crucial role in confirming the existence of atoms and molecules, which had not yet been observed under a microscope. When small particles like pollen grains are suspended in a liquid, they exhibit jittery, random motion, first observed by Robert Brown in 1827, who could not explain it. Einstein proposed that this motion resulted from numerous collisions with the molecules in the fluid, which are invisible to the naked eye but constantly in motion due to thermal energy. He mathematically demonstrated that the seemingly irregular movement of visible particles was the result of countless collisions with fast-moving, invisible molecules. Einstein also provided a method to calculate the displacement of a suspended particle over time, depending on factors like temperature, viscosity, and particle size. While the idea of atoms had existed since ancient times, it was not universally accepted. With this work, Einstein provided a robust, quantitative argument for their existence, bridging the gap between physics and chemistry and advancing the field of statistical mechanics.

In June 1905, Einstein published "On the Electrodynamics of Moving Bodies," a revolutionary paper that transformed our understanding of time, space, and motion. This paper introduced the concept of special relativity and laid the groundwork for general relativity. James Clerk Maxwell had shown that light travels at the same speed for all observers, which puzzled physicists. No matter how fast one travels, light appears to move at the same speed. This contradicts our everyday experiences—when sitting in a car, stationary trees seem to whizz by, while passengers appear to be at rest relative to us. This relative motion inspired Einstein's special theory of relativity. He devised a thought experiment

involving a man bouncing a ball of light on a moving train while another man observed from the platform. Without delving too deeply into the physics, Einstein realized that time and space are relative. He concluded that time slows down for objects moving at high speeds relative to an observer, causing them to appear shorter than they are. While this effect is negligible at everyday speeds, it becomes significant at speeds close to the speed of light.

Later, Einstein expanded his theory into the general theory of relativity, providing a deeper understanding of the universe.

In September 1905, Einstein published a brief paper on mass-energy equivalence, which introduced his most famous equation, $E=mc^2$. Let's break down this groundbreaking equation that reveals the secret nature of all matter. In this equation, E stands for energy, m for mass, and c represents the speed of light in a vacuum (approximately 3 × 10^8 m/s). This equation is revolutionary because it shows that mass and energy are interchangeable—two sides of the same coin. All matter possesses inherent energy that can be converted to and from mass, quantified by this equation. Although we don't typically perceive this energy on a large scale (our bodies won't simply burst into energy), the conversion is profound. For instance, just one kilogram of mass can release about 9 × 10^16 joules of energy—equivalent to the energy of 21.5 million tons of TNT. This principle is practically applied in nuclear reactors, where small particles like atoms and electrons are converted into energy. It is also the mechanism behind the sun's energy production, as it converts a small portion of atomic mass into energy, and it played a role in the development of atomic weapons.

In summary, within a single year, Einstein provided humanity with a concrete understanding of matter, energy, space, time, and subatomic particles. Without his work, our knowledge would be considerably diminished, and many of our technological advancements would not exist.

My inspiration — The man who was the Genius

46

How does calculus work?

Calculus may seem like a daunting subject—the pinnacle of high school mathematics and a culmination of various topics studied throughout the years. Given its importance, it must be quite complicated, right? Surprisingly, the basic concept calculus tackles is inherently simple. Let's explore this further.

The history of calculus spans nearly two millennia, making it far from a recent development. The Ancient Greeks and Indians first laid the groundwork for calculus. Archimedes approximated the value of pi and calculated the volume of various shapes using an early form of calculus known as the method of exhaustion. The philosopher Zeno created paradoxes that could only be resolved with an understanding of calculus. Indian mathematicians like Aryabhata and Bhaskara II also engaged in rudimentary forms of calculus to solve astronomical problems. Over the years, calculus evolved, reaching its refinement through the work of Isaac Newton and Gottfried Leibniz. Let's understand how they defined this mysterious concept.

Calculus is of 3 fundamental forms, limits, differentiation, and integration. These are operations that act on a function to understand how it behaves. A function is simply a relation of the variable x, which can take any number – x^2 is a function, and so is 5x+7. Essentially, it can be thought of a machine, where one inputs a number for x and out pops the respective number for that x. The relation between the output and input is the function. If my function is x^3, then inputting the number 3 will output 27, while inputting the number -2, we will get -8 as the output. We often graph these functions on a grid, with the vertical axis representing the output and horizontal axis, the input. Put geometrically, a limit is what the output of a function should be for a certain output when that output is actually undefined (undefined values come from division by 0 and other mathematical impossibilities). A derivative is the slope of the function graph and integration calculates the area under the graph. Now this is all seems quite mathematical and abstract, so let's put it into perspective.

Consider the study of a rabbit population in an ecosystem. Rabbits reproduce rapidly, leading to an initial population surge. However, there must always be a balance in any ecosystem; natural resources cannot support infinite growth. Consequently, the rabbit population will eventually level off. When plotting the number of rabbits against time, we might be interested in the final population that the ecosystem can sustain. To determine this, we use the concept of limits. Since calculating an infinite amount of time is impossible, we examine what value the graph approaches as time approaches infinity. This value gives us the limit of the function as it approaches infinity. This is just one of many applications, but it illustrates the fundamental concept well.

Next, let's explore derivatives or differentiation. Imagine a car driving down a city road, exceeding the speed limit and getting caught by a speed camera. The camera works by taking two pictures within a certain time interval. By measuring the distance the car moved during that time and dividing it by the time taken, the camera can calculate the car's speed.

However, suppose the camera is faulty and takes the two pictures a minute apart. In court, the driver argues that he was slowing down; although he was slightly over the speed limit when the first picture was taken, he was well under it by the time of the second picture. It becomes challenging to discern the driver's exact, instantaneous speed at the moment he crossed the camera.

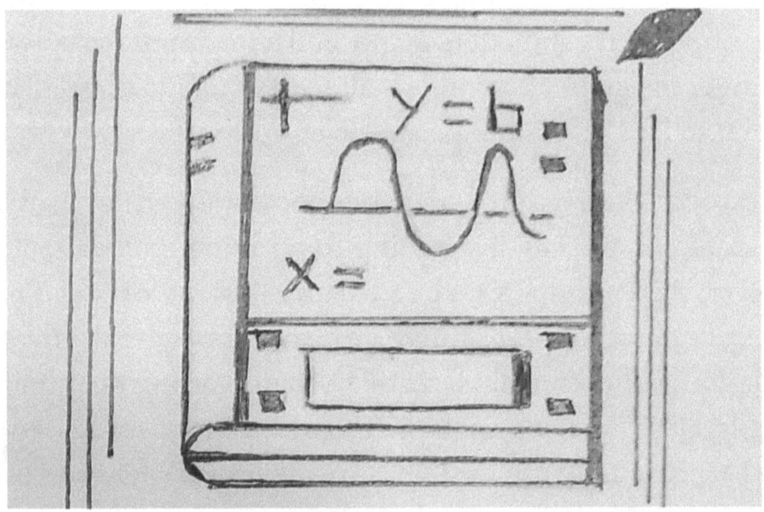

Its really not that complex

To achieve a more accurate reading, the pictures could be taken closer together in time—say, within a second. This would provide a better estimate of speed, but still not an exact measurement. To find the precise speed when the car crossed the camera, we would need an infinitely small window between the two pictures. By calculating the infinitesimal distance moved between these frames, we could determine the instantaneous velocity. There are mathematical techniques to find this velocity without having to take two infinitely fast pictures. This method of finding the instantaneous rate of change of a function (in this case, the rate of change of the car's position) is called differentiation.

Finally, let's discuss integration. In mathematics classes, we often explore arbitrary shapes with curves and jagged edges. We may be asked to approximate the area of these shapes using a square grid. If a shape fills a box completely, we would count the total area of that box; if it partially fills the box, we might count half the area. By adding up these areas, we can estimate the shape's area. However, this method only provides an approximation. By counting a box as half filled when it might actually be a quarter or third filled, we miss the exact measurement.

Naturally, the smaller the boxes, the more accurate our estimation becomes. If we only have a few boxes, we can't accurately determine the shape's area. The more numerous and smaller the boxes, the higher the accuracy. We can break up a portion of the shape that previously "half-filled" a larger box into smaller boxes, either fully or partially filled. So, what if we keep shrinking the boxes to achieve a more precise estimate? Eventually, we would reach the exact area of the shape when the boxes become infinitesimally small. This concept forms the foundation of integration. By breaking down an area into infinitely small portions and then summing them up, we can find the area of any shape. Mathematically, these infinitesimal blocks are related to a function that is used to sum them up again.

47

Why do things smell bad?

My nose doesn't really enjoy

Foul odors are everywhere—from piles of rubbish in a dustbin to stinky socks, we can't escape them. We often associate these unpleasant smells with harm, uncleanliness, and disease. But is there a reason for this? Let's delve deeper.

All smells arise from chemical compounds interacting with receptors in our nose. As molecules carried by air currents drift up our nostrils, they reach a small patch of tissue called the olfactory epithelium. Here, nerve cells are specially designed to detect these molecules and convey the sensation to our brain. Amazingly, humans have over 400 different types of olfactory receptors! Each smell we detect is a combination of signals from these receptors. The olfactory cortex of the brain then identifies the smell, while the amygdala and hippocampus contribute an emotional response and often a memory related to the smell— explaining why scents can trigger memories more powerfully than sight or hearing. The orbitofrontal cortex connects smell with taste, allowing us to experience the full flavor of our food.

But what happens when we encounter a foul odor? Malodors, with their repulsive sensation, are linked to evolutionary survival mechanisms. Common chemicals that cause malodors include sulfur compounds, amines, short-chain fatty acids, and ammonia. For example, hydrogen sulfide (the smell of rotting eggs) and mercaptans give skunks their distinctive odor. Amines are found in decaying organic matter; short-chain fatty acids are present in spoiled dairy and body odor; and ammonia is found in urine and excrement.

From an evolutionary perspective, humans have learned to avoid these smells, as they often signal disease and decay. Rotting food releases putrescine and cadaverine, compounds produced by bacteria breaking down proteins, signaling to us that the food is no longer safe to eat. Bodily excrement contains chemicals like indole, skatole, and ammonia, indicating the presence of harmful bacteria. The same applies to decaying flesh. Thus, it's not that these compounds' smells are inherently foul, but rather that we have evolved to find them repugnant. Early humans who found these smells unpleasant avoided such substances, reducing their exposure to disease and death. This subjectivity in perceiving bad odors is seen across cultures: what constitutes a foul odor can vary significantly. For example, blue cheese is a delicacy to some but unpleasant to others. Animals like vultures, which feed on decaying flesh, have evolved to ignore or perhaps even enjoy these odors.

To avoid ingesting or inhaling harmful chemicals, we often gag or scrunch our faces to block our nostrils. These reactions serve important evolutionary functions, alerting us to potential danger. Although these reactions are not always accurate—some life-saving medicines have foul odors—they play a protective role.

48

Why do we blow on tea to make it colder?

I'm sure we all have a favorite hot drink. Whether it's a comforting cup of tea, a steaming flask of coffee, or a soothing mug of hot chocolate, these drinks are indispensable. Tea is as old as time itself, with a history stretching back 5,000 years to the Chinese Empire. After oil, coffee is the second most traded commodity in the world! So, it's no wonder that each day we enjoy a cup. Whether snuggled in a cozy armchair with a book or working away at a desk, a cup of tea or coffee is always nearby. But as we know, these boiling beverages can be very hot! Right after we make one—by boiling water and adding tea leaves or coffee powder—we often set it aside to cool. We may also blow on it to speed up the cooling process. But why do we do this?

To understand the phenomenon, let's look at the process of evaporation. Blowing on our drink helps cool it down through evaporation, which is the conversion of liquid to vapor. For water molecules to evaporate, they require small amounts of energy. When molecules take away energy to evaporate, the drink's temperature lowers. As the more energetic molecules turn to vapor, the remaining energy in the liquid decreases, causing a drop in temperature.

Blowing on the surface speeds up this evaporation. It creates a gentle breeze that removes the humid air surrounding the coffee and replaces it with cooler air. When humid air becomes saturated with water vapor, it loses its ability to take in more, which slows the evaporation rate. By replacing this humid air, blowing helps keep the rate of evaporation steady. Blowing also removes surface molecules, further increasing the evaporation rate.

CaptionIf you want it cooler, blow a little faster

Another interesting effect you might notice is that the larger the surface area of the drink, the faster it cools. Tea in a cup stays hot much longer than soup in a bowl or tea spilled on a surface. This is because a larger surface area means more molecules are ready to evaporate, which speeds up evaporation. I remember my grandfather used this principle by pouring small amounts of tea into a saucer before drinking. This property also explains why we mop floors—by spreading out a spill, we enable it to dry and evaporate faster.

Of course, evaporation is not the only way tea cools down. It also loses heat to its surroundings through conduction. The hot drink warms up the cup, which in turn warms the surrounding air, causing a gradual heat loss. However, conduction is not as easily controlled—unless we surround our tea with ice cubes! Therefore, blowing on it remains the simplest and most effective way to cool it down.

49

Why does coffee help us stay awake?

Coffee is a drink we can all enjoy, whether we're feeling tired or not. It can calm us down, warm us up, and be enjoyed with milk, sugar, or even black. Coffee has become an indispensable stimulant, loved by people all over the world. It's perfect for long working nights and an excellent way to shake off sleepiness. But how does it work?

Coffee's "secret ingredient" is caffeine, a natural stimulant. Unlike other recreational drugs, caffeine is not harmful when consumed in moderation. Although one can become dependent on it, the effects are usually mild. Caffeine works by interfering with the chemical process that makes us feel tired. To understand caffeine, we need to explore its interaction with adenosine, a chemical in the brain.

Adenosine is a neurotransmitter that builds up in the brain throughout the day, signaling us to slow down and rest when it reaches a certain level. It plays a critical role in promoting sleep and regulating our circadian rhythm. Chemically, caffeine is quite similar to adenosine.

Adenosine consists of adenine attached to a ribose sugar, and its molecular shape is similar to caffeine's purine ring. This resemblance allows caffeine to bind to adenosine receptors in the brain (specifically, the A1 and A2A receptors), effectively blocking adenosine from sending its sleep-inducing signals.

But caffeine's effects go beyond blocking adenosine. It also indirectly boosts the activity of dopamine, a neurotransmitter linked to pleasure, reward, and motivation. By increasing dopamine production, caffeine enhances focus and mental alertness. Caffeine also triggers the release of adrenaline, the "fight or flight" hormone, which increases heart rate, blood pressure, muscle power, and air passage dilation. Additionally, caffeine inhibits an enzyme called phosphodiesterase (PDE), which breaks down cyclic adenosine monophosphate (cAMP), a molecule crucial for energy production in cells. By inhibiting PDE, caffeine allows cAMP levels to remain elevated, enhancing energy production and metabolic activity. Finally, caffeine excites neurons in the brain, making them fire more rapidly, which improves reaction times and mental processing.

Another advantage of caffeine is its lasting effect. Every 4 to 6 hours, the caffeine in your body decreases by only half, as it is slowly metabolized by the liver. Depending on one's basal metabolic rate, age, and caffeine sensitivity, this rate can vary, but it generally takes a long time for caffeine to be fully processed.

The usefulness of caffeine can't be understated. By acting as a sneaky decoy for adenosine, it heightens our body's senses and boosts alertness. With few drawbacks, it's a beverage to be enjoyed—so drink on!

The first Sip — Heavenly

50

Why do we have to stir coffee?

The history of coffee spans centuries and continents, with its origins steeped in legend. Coffee can be traced back to Ethiopia, where a shepherd noticed his goats became unusually energetic after eating some red berries. When he tried the berries himself, he felt a surge of energy. These berries turned out to be coffee beans. News of this discovery spread quickly, and people soon learned that by roasting and grinding the beans, they could make a strong beverage. Unlike tea, coffee cannot be brewed by simply boiling the beans. Furthermore, to mix it properly, one must stir the ground coffee well. Let's explore why.

Coffee can only be enjoyed as a beverage once the ground beans dissolve in water. Dissolution is the process by which a solid or liquid (the solute) mixes uniformly with another liquid (the solvent) by dispersing among its molecules. For effective dissolution, the solute particles must be small. This is why we grind coffee beans before preparing the beverage. Unlike tea leaves, which readily release their soluble flavors, oils, and tannins, coffee beans are dense and less porous, binding their flavors tightly within. Grinding the beans breaks this barrier and increases the surface area of the coffee particles.

The role of the accompanying stirrer

Stirring helps dissolve coffee more quickly. If we were to leave the ground coffee in water without stirring, it would eventually dissolve, but the coffee might cool down before it's fully mixed! Stirring speeds up the dissolution process by bringing fresh solvent molecules (water) into direct contact with the coffee grounds. Without stirring, the coffee grounds interact primarily with the solvent immediately surrounding them, and dissolution proceeds slowly as each layer of solvent becomes saturated and less able to absorb more solute. Stirring disrupts this saturation and moves fresh layers of solvent to the coffee, facilitating a faster mix.

Additionally, when the solute begins to dissolve, it creates a surrounding saturated solution, making the nearby solvent less receptive to further dissolving the solute. Stirring helps to break up this saturation, allowing the solvent to take in more solute particles.

Finally, stirring increases the kinetic energy and speed of the solute particles, leading to more frequent collisions between the coffee particles and solvent molecules, which promotes faster dissolution.

51

Why can't we see atoms?

The Invisible atoms

Atoms are the building blocks of the universe. They are the basic units of matter and define the structure of everything around us. When atoms combine, they form molecules and compounds. Collections of these molecules make up the materials we see and interact with every day. However, atoms are incredibly small—around 0.1 to 0.5 nanometers in diameter. If these tiny particles make up everything we see, why can't we see them ourselves?

To understand why, let's consider how sight works. We rely on light to see objects. Sunlight brightens our world during the day, while electric lights illuminate it at night. When light hits an object, it is reflected and scattered. Some of this scattered light reaches our eyes, interacts with the optic nerve, and gives us the sensation of sight. However, atoms are smaller than the wavelength of visible light, which is about 400 to 700 nanometers—much larger than an atom. Because atoms are so small, they do not interact with visible light in the way larger objects do, and light waves simply pass by without scattering. This is why we cannot see atoms directly.

So how do scientists observe atoms? While they cannot see them with the naked eye, they use specialized techniques to produce images of them. One method involves an electron microscope, which projects beams of electrons—particles even smaller than atoms. By detecting how these electrons reflect and scatter off the atoms, scientists can generate images of them.

But this limitation goes beyond atoms. You might wonder: if we can't see atoms because they're smaller than the wavelength of light, shouldn't we be able to see everything larger than that? In theory, yes, but the smaller something is, the less likely light is to reflect off it strongly enough for us to perceive it. Consequently, objects that are too small do not reflect light with sufficient intensity to be detected by our eyes. Furthermore, the human eye has its own biological limitations. The photoreceptors in the retina can only resolve details down to about one arcminute, or 1/60th of a degree. Objects smaller than this occupy too few receptor cells to be perceived.

52

Do the atoms of an object break when we snap it?

An atom is the fundamental building block of all matter, comprising electrons and a nucleus. Electrons are subatomic particles that are even smaller than the atom itself and revolve around its nucleus, which contains protons and neutrons. Although electrons are usually bound to an atom, they still follow specific physical laws, allowing them to sometimes leave the atom under certain conditions. When atoms bond chemically, electrons are either shared or transferred between them. In electrically conducting materials, electrons are shared across the entire substance.

However, when we break or drop an object, atoms and electrons do not fall out in the traditional sense.

Let's start with a few definitions. A molecule is a group of atoms held together by strong forces known as chemical bonds. An object consists of many such molecules, connected by these bonds. The strength of these bonds depends on the chemical properties of the substance. The stronger the bond, the harder it is to break and separate the object. When we do break an object, we only disrupt the bonds (or forces) between molecules. It's virtually impossible to break the bonds between individual atoms or split the atoms themselves through physical means. The only practical way to break atomic bonds is through chemical reactions, which utilize atoms' natural tendencies and desire for stability. To split the atom itself requires nuclear reactions, which release immense energy. Therefore, breaking objects typically means separating clusters of molecules rather than individual atoms.

The atoms snapped

But there's more! Electrons can also be removed by physical means alone. For example, running a comb through dry hair or rubbing hard rubber with a silk cloth displaces electrons, a phenomenon known as charging by friction. You can try it yourself: comb your hair for a while, then bring the comb near small pieces of paper, and you'll see them attracted to it. Only certain materials, called insulators, can be charged by friction. When two materials are rubbed together, electrons jump from one material to the other; one material has a stronger "desire" for electrons than the other. Consequently, one material gains a positive charge (by losing electrons), while the other gains a negative charge (by gaining electrons). This simple method allows us to interact with the microscopic, subatomic world in surprising ways.

53

What makes things sweet?

Sweet treats are our guilty pleasure—cakes, chocolates, candies...the list goes on. A meal often feels incomplete without a good dessert. Even our ancestors recognized the allure of sweets: the ancient Egyptians made honey cakes and candies from dates, figs, and nuts to offer to the gods. The Greeks and Romans loved pastries flavored with honey, cheese, wine, dried fruits, and nuts. Over time, desserts evolved with the addition of cocoa, spices, and sugar, becoming the delightful treats we know today. But why do we enjoy them so much, and why do we usually have them after our main course instead of before?

Let's start by understanding how we taste sweetness. Sweet substances primarily consist of sugars like glucose, fructose, and sucrose, which all have similar structures of carbon, hydrogen, and oxygen atoms. Glucose is found in carbohydrates, like bread, which may not taste sweet at first but will if you chew it long enough. Fructose is found in fruits, while sucrose is the common sugar we use in cooking. Much of the food we eat consists of complex carbohydrates that break down into simpler sugars with the help of amylase, an enzyme in our saliva. Sweetness is detected by taste buds spread across the tongue, contrary to the myth of specific "taste zones." When a sweet substance contacts T1R2 and T1R3 receptors on the taste buds, they send signals to the brain that register as sweetness. Artificial sweeteners like aspartame, saccharin, and sucralose also trigger these receptors, though they pass through the body without providing as many calories.

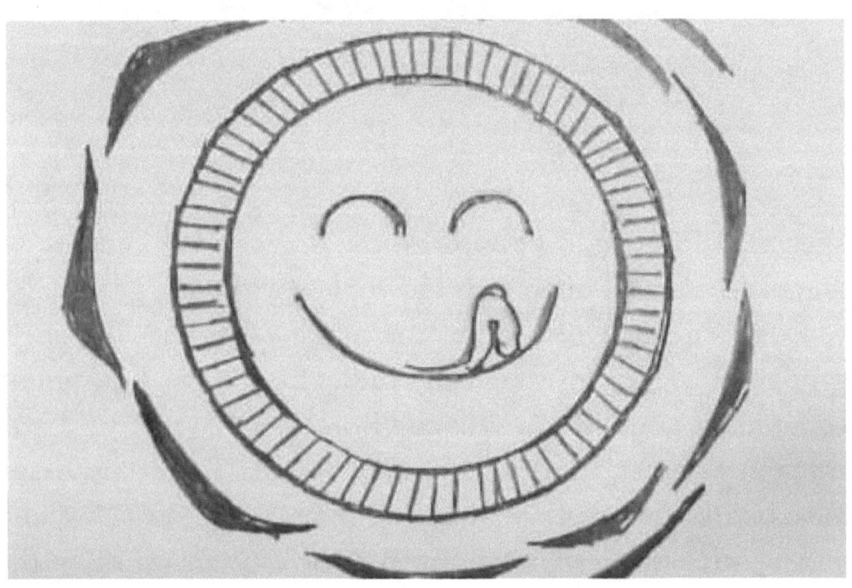

Ice creams and Cream Cakes - -and Beyond

Our preference for sweetness is shaped by evolution. While animals may not perceive sweetness exactly as we do, most are naturally drawn to high-energy foods. Birds are attracted to ripe fruits, and horses have a notable fondness for sugar. A whale given sugar cubes might perceive them as bitter, but for humans and other animals, sweet foods signal energy and nutrients.

So, why do we typically have sweets after our main course? The custom of enjoying dessert at the end of a meal has biological, psychological, and cultural roots. Sugar activates the brain's reward system by releasing dopamine—the neurotransmitter associated with pleasure and satisfaction. Eating something sweet after a meal enhances enjoyment, giving a sense of completion. Additionally, the contrast of sweetness after a savory main course provides a refreshing change, cleansing the palate and adding variety to the meal. Some researchers suggest that cravings for sugar post-meal may stem from a dip in glucose levels. As the body digests food and releases insulin to regulate blood sugar, we may crave sweets to restore balance. Over time, these factors have cemented dessert as a perfect after-meal indulgence.

54

How are clothes made?

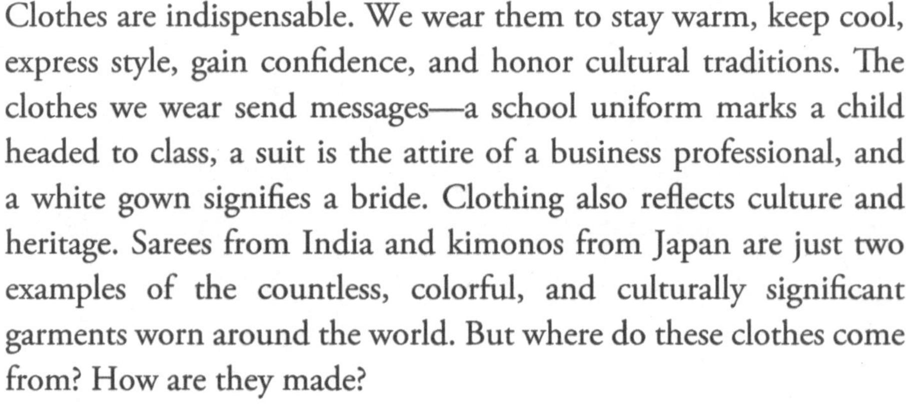

Clothes are indispensable. We wear them to stay warm, keep cool, express style, gain confidence, and honor cultural traditions. The clothes we wear send messages—a school uniform marks a child headed to class, a suit is the attire of a business professional, and a white gown signifies a bride. Clothing also reflects culture and heritage. Sarees from India and kimonos from Japan are just two examples of the countless, colorful, and culturally significant garments worn around the world. But where do these clothes come from? How are they made?

The history of clothing production stretches back tens of thousands of years. Early clothing was primarily functional, designed to shield people from the elements. Prehistoric humans wore animal skins and furs to protect themselves from harsh weather. Archaeologists have even found sewing tools dating back 40,000 years, indicating that humans have been sewing since the Stone Age. With the rise of agriculture, people began cultivating plants specifically for textiles, such as flax and cotton. The invention of the loom enabled the production of linen from flax, which is light and breathable—ideal for warm regions like Egypt and

Mesopotamia. In colder areas, wool from sheep fleece became common. As civilizations evolved, so did clothing, and garments increasingly became symbols of status. Nobility wore luxurious fabrics like velvet, while peasants typically donned wool and linen. The Renaissance era saw a surge in fashion innovation, with new techniques like embroidery, lacemaking, and dyeing adding beauty and intricacy to clothing. The Industrial Revolution later introduced mass production, shaping the modern clothing industry.

The clothes manufacturing process

Making clothes is a multi-step process, which varies based on fabric type and complexity but generally follows a consistent structure. First, raw materials are gathered to create the fabric, ranging from natural fibers like cotton, wool, and silk, to synthetic fibers like polyester and nylon derived from petrochemicals. Once obtained, raw fibers are straightened, cleaned, and spun into yarn or thread. Next, the yarn is either woven or knitted into fabric. In weaving, threads are interlaced in a perpendicular grid pattern, a task performed on a loom. Knitting, on the other hand, involves looping yarn together to create stretchy, elastic fabrics. Once the fabric is made, it's dyed for color. Often, fabrics go through additional finishing processes to enhance durability, such as softening, waterproofing, or flameproofing. Finally, the fabric is cut and sewn to create the final garment. After a quality check, garments are shipped to stores.

Today, most of these processes are automated, with machines playing a significant role in production. However, we should remember the artisans and handicraft workers who pour dedication and skill into each handmade piece—a reminder of the art and soul in clothing creation.

55

What do the channels on a radio mean?

A car journey feels incomplete without the radio. As a child, I fondly remember singing along to songs in my father's car, making road trips all the more enjoyable. Sometimes, I'd discover a new favorite song that I'd later play on repeat. Even the advertisements and skits on air were captivating and often brought a smile to my face. But one thing that puzzled me was the numbers on the radio. Each station was marked with a seemingly random decimal. Why would a channel choose to be "99.2 FM" instead of "100 FM"? And what did "FM" even mean? Now that I know, let me share the answers with you.

A radio operates by transmitting and receiving radio waves, as the name suggests. These waves are part of the electromagnetic spectrum, which also includes microwaves (like those from a microwave oven), ultraviolet waves, and visible light. Each type of wave has a unique frequency, measured by how many times it oscillates per second. These waves carry information through these oscillations, much like how light gives us information through sight.

Radio waves, with their relatively low frequencies, are especially well-suited for communication. They travel easily through the air without much interference, don't harm the human body, and can reflect off surfaces to change direction. These properties make them ideal for radio transmission.

Tuning In

In a radio broadcast, sound waves, like voices or music, are captured by a microphone and converted into electrical signals that match the pitch and volume of the original audio. These audio signals are too weak to travel far on their own, so they're combined with radio waves in a process called modulation. There are two primary types of modulation: amplitude modulation (AM) and frequency modulation (FM). In AM, the strength, or amplitude, of the radio wave is varied to mirror the electrical signal. In FM, it's the frequency of the radio wave that changes according to the audio signal. This is where "FM" comes from. Most radio stations use frequency modulation (FM) because it offers better sound quality over short distances. AM waves, on the other hand, bounce off the Earth's ionosphere, enabling them to cover greater distances, especially at night.

Each station is identified by the primary frequency of its radio wave, which becomes the station's name. For instance, a station transmitting at 92.7 MHz is called "92.7 FM." Radio receivers, like the one in a car, are designed to pick up a specific range of frequencies from the many radio waves traveling through the air. The receiver filters out other frequencies, isolating the selected station. It then demodulates the wave, extracting the original audio by detecting the amplitude changes in AM and frequency changes in FM. Finally, this signal is sent through the speakers, bringing the audio to life.

56

How does a chameleon change colours?

Chameleons are truly fascinating creatures, renowned for their ability to change color at will. While they primarily use this remarkable skill for camouflage to evade predators, their color- changing ability serves multiple purposes. So, how do they accomplish this?

Chameleons change their colors through specialized skin cells known as chromatophores, iridophores, and melanophores. These cells interact with light and pigments to alter the chameleon's appearance. Color changes are not just for camouflage; they also play a role in communication, temperature regulation, and emotional expression.

Chromatophores are located in the upper layers of the chameleon's skin and contain various colored pigments. The arrangement of these pigments determines the chameleon's base color. Beneath the chromatophores lie the iridophores, which expand the chameleon's color palette. These cells reflect light using nanocrystals of guanine, producing shades of white or blue.

Finally, melanophores contain melanin, a pigment that darkens the chameleon's color.

But how do chameleons manipulate these cells? They can control the spacing of the nanocrystals in the iridophores and the arrangement of pigments in the chromatophores. By expanding or contracting their iridophores, they change the way light is reflected. Closely packed nanocrystals reflect shorter wavelengths, creating blue hues, while more spaced-out crystals reflect longer wavelengths, resulting in red tones. The combination of these wavelengths with the pigments determines the chameleon's final color.

Captivating Colours

So, why do chameleons change color in the first place? Their color often reflects their emotional state, with bright, vivid colors signaling aggression and muted tones indicating calmness. Color is also used to attract potential mates or intimidate rivals. Additionally, as cold-blooded animals, chameleons use color to regulate their body temperature. Darker colors absorb more heat, helping them stay warm, while brighter colors reflect sunlight, keeping them cool. Finally, their camouflage helps them hide from predators, a tactic that, as many videos online demonstrate, is highly effective.

57

Why is cotton soft and wood hard?

We have all experienced the softness of cotton clothes and the cold rigidity of a wooden table. The light, smooth feathers of a bird contrast sharply with the solid nature of iron. But why are some materials strong while others are malleable?

The hardness of an object is fundamentally linked to its atomic and molecular structure, specifically how strongly the particles of the material are bonded together. All matter is composed of atoms, which vary in size and properties, and these atoms combine to form molecules. Each compound on Earth is associated with a specific molecular structure. For example, a carbon dioxide molecule consists of two oxygen atoms bonded to a central carbon atom. The atoms and molecules are held together by bonds—both atomic and intermolecular. The strength, type, and arrangement of these bonds largely determine the hardness of a material.

Atomic bonds can primarily be ionic or covalent. Ionic bonds occur when one atom donates an electron to another, forming a strong bond between them. In contrast, covalent bonds are created when two atoms share electrons. In metals, atoms share a "sea" of free-flowing electrons, which allows them to shift position slightly without breaking the overall structure, imparting both hardness and flexibility.

Intermolecular forces, while not as strong as atomic bonds, are also crucial to a material's integrity. These forces include van der Waals forces, hydrogen bonds, and weaker ionic bonds. If a material has weak intermolecular forces, it takes less energy to move the molecules around, making it easier to deform. Harder materials typically have stronger intermolecular forces, which resist deformation.

Soft and Hard Matters

Another important characteristic contributing to a material's strength is its crystalline structure. Materials like diamonds, metals, and certain minerals have an organized pattern of molecules known as a crystal lattice. This stable arrangement makes these materials difficult to deform. In contrast, amorphous structures, like glass or rubber, feature molecules arranged in a random, irregular order, rendering them more flexible and softer. This effect is even more pronounced in fluids (liquids or gases), where the molecules are disordered, random, and held together by very weak intermolecular forces, allowing them to take the shape of their container.

Some materials are soft due to their loosely packed nature. For instance, foams and sponges contain numerous air pockets, while gelatin has protein molecules that form a loose network to trap water.

Finally, we have elastic materials, like rubber, which are somewhat of an anomaly in the world of matter. They deform easily but return to their original shape immediately. This property arises from the flexibility of their molecular chains. Rubber is composed of polymer chains—repeating structures of carbon and hydrogen—that stretch under force but are loose enough to spring back into shape once the force is removed..

58

Where does our water come from?

The origins of life

Water is essential to life, and all animals require it to survive. This simple molecule, H_2O, plays a critical role in both fauna and flora. Beyond drinking, we need water for countless purposes. It shapes our planet and supports ecosystems in numerous ways, filling oceans, lakes, rivers, and streams; flowing through the atmosphere as vapor; forming clouds; and falling back to Earth as rain and snow. Below the surface, it seeps through soil and rocks, sustaining plants and entire ecosystems. Despite covering 71% of the Earth's surface, only about 0.3% of this water is usable. Let's explore where this water comes from.

Interestingly, a significant portion of Earth's water is believed to have originated from space, particularly from comets and asteroids that collided with the planet during its early formation. Additionally, intense volcanic activity in Earth's history released water vapor from the planet's molten interior. As Earth cooled, this vapor condensed into liquid, forming oceans, rivers, and lakes. Water is continuously recycled through the hydrological cycle: it evaporates from oceans and lakes into the atmosphere, condenses to form clouds, and eventually precipitates back to the surface.

But how does this water reach our homes?

Water is supplied to households through a complex underground system, primarily sourced from surface water (rivers, lakes, and reservoirs) and groundwater (from aquifers, which are underground layers of rock and soil that store water). While most cities and towns depend on surface water, many rural areas rely on groundwater accessed through deep wells.

Before water reaches our taps, it undergoes several treatment steps to ensure it is clean and safe to drink. The specific process may vary depending on the water source and local infrastructure, but the general steps are as follows:

1. **Coagulation**: Chemicals are added to clump together small particles like dirt, algae, and organic matter.
2. **Sedimentation**: The clumps formed during coagulation settle at the bottom of the treatment tank.

3. **Filtration**: The water is passed through filters made of sand, gravel, and activated carbon to remove smaller impurities.
4. **Disinfection**: Chlorine, ozone, or UV light are used to kill harmful bacteria, viruses, and parasites.

Once treated, the water is stored in large reservoirs or towers to ensure a steady supply. Pumping stations distribute the water from treatment plants to storage facilities. A vast network of pipes delivers water to homes, equipped with valves to control flow. The pressure within these pipes is carefully regulated to prevent damage.

When the water reaches our homes, it flows through a main supply pipe and is distributed to various fixtures, such as showers, taps, and heaters.

59

Where does electricity come from?

Electricity is the cornerstone of modern technology. Without our ability to harness the flow of electrons, we wouldn't have the technological advancements that define our daily lives.

Electricity powers our homes, devices, gadgets, and appliances, but where does it come from?

Let's first discuss how electricity is produced. Electricity can be generated from various sources by transforming energy from natural resources into electrical energy. The most common sources of electricity are fossil fuels—coal, oil, and natural gas. These fuels are burned to produce steam, which drives turbines to generate electricity. In nuclear power plants, the atoms of uranium or plutonium are split in a process called fission, releasing tremendous amounts of energy. This energy is used to produce steam that rotates turbines, similar to fossil fuel power generation.

Turbines generate electricity through the principle of electromagnetic induction. When a magnet rotates, it produces an electric current in nearby wires. These turbines are connected to large magnets that spin to produce a strong electric current. Renewable energy sources, such as hydroelectric dams and windmills, utilize the same principle to harness natural elements to rotate their turbines.

Once electricity is generated, it must be transported over long distances to reach our homes. To do this efficiently, the voltage is increased using a step-up transformer. A step-up transformer consists of two parallel sets of coils with a different number of loops. Through electromagnetic induction, one set of coils induces a current in the other set. By changing the ratio of coils, the voltage produced can be increased. Higher voltage is necessary for long-distance travel to minimize energy loss.

The Electrical Generator

The electricity is then transmitted through high-voltage transmission lines, the long power lines that stretch across landscapes. Upon reaching a local distribution area, the voltage must be reduced for safe consumption. Step-down transformers accomplish this through a reverse process. The electricity is then carried by smaller power lines called distribution lines, which deliver it to homes, schools, and businesses. Finally, electricity enters our homes through a service drop, ready for use.

60

Where does our waste go?

Disposing off the unwanted

After receiving a parcel, we often carelessly toss the box in the bin, along with potato peels, onion skins, and apple cores. Anything we've used or discarded is quickly thrown away without a second thought. But what happens to this waste once it leaves our sight?

The journey of our waste depends on its type and the waste management systems in our area. After neatly tying our waste in a trash bag, it is collected by the municipality. Most household trash is then either dumped in a landfill, incinerated, or recycled.

Landfills are large designated areas where waste is buried. They are the most common method of waste disposal worldwide. In a landfill, waste is layered and engineered to minimize environmental harm. Liners are installed to prevent harmful chemicals from leaching into groundwater and soil, and leachate collection systems gather any liquid squeezed out of the waste for treatment. It's crucial to capture the methane released during decomposition, as it serves as a valuable energy source. However, landfills have drawbacks; if not managed properly, they can release greenhouse gases and cause contamination. As available space for landfills diminishes, we turn to our next waste management process: **incineration**.

Incineration involves burning waste at high temperatures to reduce its volume, and the heat generated can be used to produce electricity. If you've seen the Pixar movie "Toy Story 3," you might recall the terrifying scene in the incinerator plant, which accurately depicts this process. Waste is burned in large furnaces and often compressed beforehand. Scrubbers and filters are employed to minimize the release of pollutants. However, while incineration reduces waste size and produces energy, it also generates carbon dioxide and toxins, which can pose environmental concerns.

Lastly, we have **recycling**, which reprocesses waste into new products. For instance, paper is turned into pulp and recycled into new paper products, while plastics are transformed into raw materials for creating other plastic items. Glass and metals are melted down and reshaped, and organic waste can be converted into compost or fertilizer. However, recyclable materials must be separated from non-recyclable ones, either at the household level or at a materials recovery facility. Before recycling, materials are cleaned and processed. This method saves energy, decreases landfill use, and reduces our reliance on raw materials, making it the best option when possible.

You may wonder, "What happens to the water from taps?" Rather than ending up in a landfill, wastewater is managed through sewage systems. These pipes transport wastewater to treatment plants, where large solids are removed through screening and sedimentation (allowing heavy particles to settle at the bottom). Beneficial bacteria and microorganisms then break down organic matter. Finally, the water is filtered and disinfected with chlorine or UV light. The treated water can either be released into rivers and oceans or reused for irrigation.

It's also important to note that **hazardous waste**—toxic, flammable, or corrosive materials— cannot be disposed of through the methods mentioned above. Instead, this waste is collected separately to be neutralized. Chemical treatment removes harmful properties, after which it may be incinerated or sent to landfills.

And that's how our waste disappears from under our noses!

61

How does medicine work?

Medicine plays a crucial role in our well-being. It alleviates pain, alleviates symptoms, and combats the pathogens that threaten our health. The development of medicine has significantly increased the average life expectancy, making it an indispensable part of our lives. But how exactly does it work?

There are several types of medicine, each designed to combat specific conditions in the body. Doctors, trained to identify symptoms and diagnose diseases, prescribe various medications, including antibiotics, pain relievers (analgesics), antivirals, vaccines, antidepressants, blood pressure medications, and insulin.

Antibiotics are designed to fight bacterial infections by either killing bacteria or inhibiting their growth. They target specific parts of bacteria, such as the cell wall or protein production centers, without harming human cells. However, antibiotics cannot distinguish between harmful and beneficial bacteria, often disrupting the digestive bacteria in our gut and leading to digestive issues after a course of antibiotics. A well-known example of an antibiotic is penicillin.

Pain relievers, known as analgesics, are essential for managing severe pain from infections or surgical procedures. These medications work by interfering with the transmission of pain signals to the brain. Common non-steroidal anti-inflammatory drugs (NSAIDs), like ibuprofen and aspirin, inhibit the COX-1 and COX-2 enzymes responsible for pain and inflammation. In cases of extreme pain, such as during amputations, **anesthetics** or **opioids** are used. These substances bind to opioid receptors in the brain and spinal cord, numbing specific areas and reducing pain perception.

Antiviral drugs treat viral infections by inhibiting the virus's ability to replicate. They prevent the virus from entering host cells and block its genetic material from copying, which is crucial for its invasion. For example, **Tamiflu** inhibits the proteins required by the flu virus to spread.

Not all diseases are physical; **antidepressants** are crucial for treating depression and related mental illnesses, such as anxiety disorders or panic attacks. They alter brain chemistry by influencing chemicals known as neurotransmitters, which regulate mood and emotions.

Among various antidepressants, **Selective Serotonin Reuptake Inhibitors (SSRIs)** are the most common, as they increase serotonin levels by preventing its reabsorption, thereby improving mood.

Blood pressure medications (antihypertensives) manage high blood pressure by affecting the circulatory system. They block the production of the angiotensin hormone, which narrows blood vessels. Without angiotensin, blood vessels widen, reducing blood pressure. **Diuretics** also play a role by eliminating excess salt and water, decreasing the volume of blood the heart must pump.

Finally, you may have heard about **insulin**, especially in relation to diabetes. Insulin is a hormone that helps maintain blood sugar levels by enabling cells to absorb glucose, which provides energy. In people with diabetes, insulin production is impaired, necessitating external insulin injections to manage blood sugar levels.

Medicines typically work in four ways:

1. **Binding to receptors**: Medications interact with specific cell receptors, changing how the cell behaves. For instance, beta-blockers bind to heart receptors, slowing the heart rate and reducing blood pressure.

2. **Inhibiting enzymes**: Some medications inhibit enzymes in the body, affecting various biochemical processes.

3. **Altering chemical signals**: Antidepressants modify neurotransmitter activity, helping regulate mood and emotional response.

4. **Replacing hormones**: Conditions caused by hormone deficiencies (like hypothyroidism or diabetes) are treated with medications that replace or supplement those hormones.

Different medicines enter the body through various routes, ultimately reaching the bloodstream. Once inside, they are transported to specific organs, guided by their chemical structure. After performing their function, medicines are broken down by the liver and excreted through the kidneys

Pills plying in our system

62

Why do we look like our parents?

Understanding Genetics: The Science of Inheritance

From the moment we are born, we exhibit traits that resemble those of our parents. For instance, if both of our parents have dark hair, it's likely that we will too. Characteristics such as eye color, nose shape, hair color, body type, and even aspects of our personality can often be traced back to our genetic heritage. However, while we may share similarities with our siblings, each of us is unique. But why is this the case?

The answer lies in our **genes**. The study of inherited traits and genes is known as **genetics**. At the core of genetics is **DNA** (Deoxyribonucleic Acid), a molecule composed of two long strands that coil around each other to form a **double helix**. These strands are connected by smaller units called **nucleotides**, which carry the instructions for the development, functioning, and reproduction of all living beings. The sequence of nucleotides dictates the production of proteins, which in turn influences how each part of the body develops.

DNA is tightly packed into structures known as **chromosomes**. A typical human cell contains **23 pairs** of chromosomes, while a butterfly cell might have as many as **380**! Each chromosome holds thousands of **genes**, segments of DNA that are responsible for specific traits. The specific arrangement of nucleotides serves as a code, with each snippet corresponding to a particular feature, such as hair color, height, blood type, risk of disease, or personality. Each person inherits two copies of every gene—one from their mother and one from their father. Depending on which gene is dominant, a particular trait will manifest.

Inheritance occurs through a process called **meiosis**. In this process, reproductive cells from each parent carry half of their genetic information and merge to form an embryo. As a result, all offspring inherit half of their DNA from each parent. Humans have one pair of sex chromosomes (X and Y) that determine biological sex, while the remaining 22 pairs carry other genetic information. During reproduction, the chromosomes from the parents recombine and shuffle, creating a unique mix of traits. This genetic reshuffling is why we are distinct from our siblings.

However, genes are not the sole determinants of who we are. **Epigenetics** refers to the interaction between our genes and the environment, allowing certain genes to be turned "on" or "off." While we cannot alter our DNA sequence, environmental factors—such as diet, stress, and exposure to toxins—can lead to epigenetic changes. This explains why identical twins, who share the same DNA, may still exhibit slight differences in their traits.

In summary, we inherit traits from our parents through the combination of their genes. The specific arrangement of nucleotide sequences, along with epigenetic factors, instructs our body's cells on how to develop, resulting in the unique characteristics that define each of us.

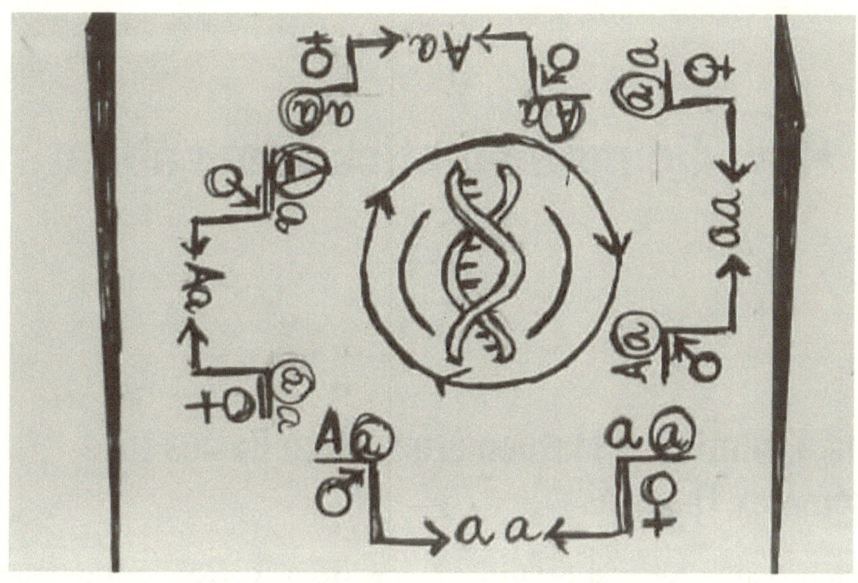

Me, my father and my mother

63

How did mathematics come about?

The Evolution of Mathematics: From Basics to Complex Theories

Mathematics is a vast field that ranges from everyday arithmetic to advanced linear algebra. Many students find themselves intimidated or bored in math classes, often questioning its practical applications. However, mathematics is essential in every branch of science, including physics, statistics, and even psychology. Its history is rich, reflecting humanity's journey through the ages. Let's explore how mathematics began.

The origins of mathematics are deeply intertwined with the development of human civilization. It emerged as a practical tool for solving everyday problems, such as counting and measuring. Over time, it evolved into an abstract discipline focused on logical reasoning, patterns, and the fundamental structure of our universe. Early humans likely grasped basic mathematical concepts, a capability shared by many organisms that display counting and measuring skills. A prehistoric artifact known as the **Ishango bone**, dating back 20,000 years, features notches that may represent counting. Early systems of tally marks and counting with stones were developed to track goods, livestock, and populations. Additionally, early civilizations required geometry for land measurement, understanding how to divide land accurately.

As human societies grew more complex, so too did their mathematical systems. Around **3000 BCE**, the Babylonians developed a sophisticated number system based on **sexagesimal** (base-60) principles, which is why we still use 60 seconds in a minute and 360 degrees in a circle today. They possessed knowledge of multiplication, division, quadratic equations, and basic trigonometry. The **Plimpton 322** tablet shows that they understood the Pythagorean theorem long before Pythagoras.

The ancient Egyptians employed mathematics for practical purposes, such as land measurement, tax calculation, and building design. The **Pyramids of Giza** stand as a testament to their mastery of geometry and trigonometry. They were the first to use fractions and developed early forms of algebra. Ancient Chinese mathematicians contributed to arithmetic, notably developing the decimal system we use today and inventing the **abacus**.

Between **600 BCE** and **300 CE**, the ancient Greeks transformed mathematics into a more abstract and theoretical discipline. They recognized the need to prove concepts that seemed self-evident. **Euclid**, often referred to as the father of geometry, wrote *The Elements* around **300 BCE**. This 13-book work systematically compiled the knowledge of geometry and number theory of his time and remained a textbook for centuries. Euclid pioneered the use of axioms and proofs, starting from basic definitions—such as defining a point as infinitely small and a line as the shortest distance between two points—to prove more complex theorems. **Archimedes** also made significant contributions to geometry, providing deeper insights into volumes and shapes, and laying the groundwork for calculus.

The contributions of Indian and Islamic mathematicians are equally significant. One of the most crucial discoveries was the concept of **zero** in number theory. While it may seem obvious now, it was the Indian mathematician **Aryabhata**who introduced the concept of nothingness to the mathematical realm. He also made important discoveries in algebra and trigonometry. **Brahmagupta** later developed rules governing the use of zero, including its addition and multiplication with other numbers.

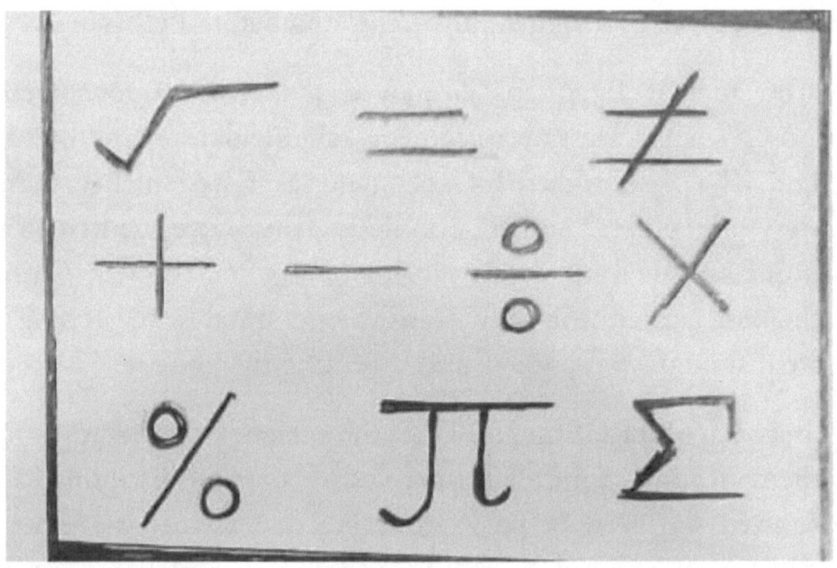

The simple formulae

During the **Islamic Golden Age**, mathematicians preserved and expanded upon the knowledge of the Greeks, Indians, and Babylonians, which had been lost to the Western world during the Middle Ages. **Al-Khwarizmi**, known as the father of algebra, introduced systematic methods for solving equations. The term

algorithm is derived from his name. Islamic mathematicians also developed trigonometric tables and introduced the sine, cosine, and tangent functions.

The revival of science and mathematics during the **Renaissance** sparked a wave of pioneering developments in the Western world. **René Descartes** introduced the Cartesian coordinate system, laying the foundation for analytical geometry. **Isaac Newton** and **Gottfried Leibniz** are credited with the development of calculus, a fundamental aspect of modern mathematics. In the **20th century**, the rise of computers revolutionized mathematics, leading to significant advancements in computer science and cryptography, which now play crucial roles in our world.

64

Why does it rain?

Pitter-Patter Raindrops

The Dual Nature of Rain: Rain can be both a blessing and a curse. At times, it provides relief from scorching heat; at others, it washes away everything we hold dear. It nourishes our crops but can also flood them in an instant. The rain from the heavens is terrifying yet awe-inspiring. When a cloud bursts into a deafening downpour, its sound resonates across the land. But where does this rain come from? Why does it only rain when the sky is cloudy?

Rain is part of the Earth's natural water cycle, which is the continuous movement of water between the Earth's surface and the atmosphere. Water from oceans, lakes, rivers, and other large bodies evaporates into the atmosphere, transforming from liquid to water vapor due to the heat of the sun. Additionally, plants contribute to this process through **transpiration**, releasing water vapor from tiny pores in their leaves. This vapor, being lighter than air, rises into the atmosphere.

As the water vapor ascends, the air temperature decreases. Higher layers of the atmosphere are less dense and have less energy compared to the denser, warmer air at lower altitudes. This is why the summit of Mt. Everest, despite being near the tropics, is covered in snow.

As the water vapor rises, it cools down and eventually condenses into tiny droplets of liquid. These droplets clump together, forming the clouds we observe in the sky. When the droplets grow too large or heavy to remain suspended, they fall back to Earth as **precipitation**.

Depending on atmospheric conditions at the time, this precipitation can take the form of snow, sleet, hail, or rain. The rain seeps into the ground, replenishing lakes and oceans while nourishing plants, thus starting the cycle anew.

65

Why do we get hurt?

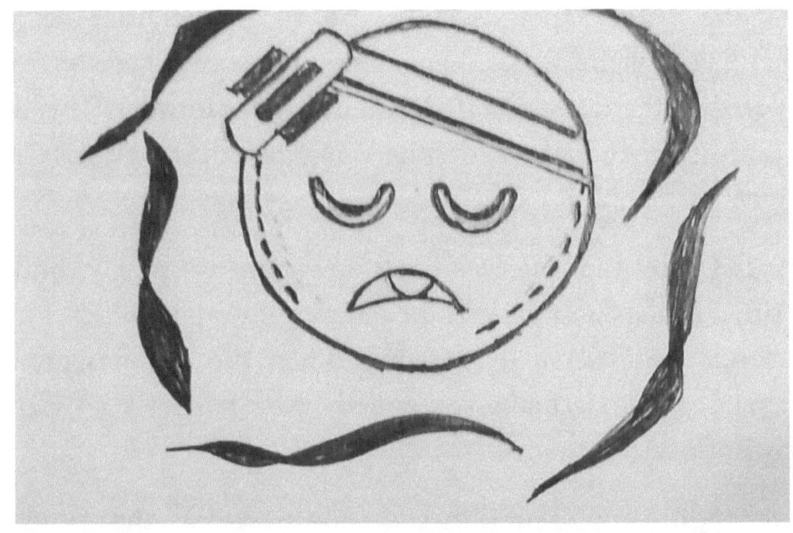

Ouch ! It Hurts

Understanding Pain: A Natural Defense Mechanism

Accidents are a natural part of life. We all experience pain at some point, whether from falling and bruising our knees, cutting ourselves while chopping vegetables, or even breaking a bone. The pain we feel can be immeasurable, so why do we experience it?

Our bodies are relatively frail and subjected to daily wear and tear. While our skin protects us from dust, wind, cold, and other elements, it is not impervious to all injuries. Cuts and bruises illustrate this fragility; they result from damage to the skin, which causes bleeding when blood vessels are exposed. Fortunately, these wounds heal as fibrinogen in the blood converts to fibrin, forming a clot over the injury. The reason we feel pain, however, is due to the body's defense mechanism.

Pain serves as a crucial signal, alerting us that something is wrong and protecting us from further harm. For instance, individuals with **CIPA (Congenital Insensitivity to Pain with Anhidrosis)** are unable to feel pain or temperature sensations. They must constantly monitor their bodies for cuts and bruises to ensure their safety, demonstrating the vital role pain plays in our lives.

It's also essential to recognize that pain is not solely physical. Our emotional and psychological states can influence how we perceive pain. Factors like stress and fear can exacerbate the sensation of pain, signaling to us that we should remove ourselves from harmful situations.

When our body experiences external injury or damage, specialized nerve endings known as **nociceptors** are activated. These nociceptors are responsible for sensing potential threats to our tissues, such as excessive heat, pressure, or chemical changes. Upon detecting damage, nociceptors send electrical signals to the spinal cord and brain, which process these signals and interpret them as pain.

In some cases, particularly when an immediate response is needed, a reflexive neural pathway is utilized. In these situations, signals travel only to the spinal cord, which makes a quick decision to protect the body. A common example is the reflex action of withdrawing your hand after touching a hot surface.

The intensity of pain correlates with the strength of the stimulus and the level of caution required. Consequently, pain primarily acts as a warning system, protecting us from further injury and informing us that the wounded area needs time to heal.

66

How does art convey a message?

The Profound Impact of Art: A Journey Through Color and Meaning

Art is a remarkable concept that enriches our lives and fuels creativity. Without it, life would be dull, and the expression of human experience would suffer. From the earliest cave paintings created by humans to the sophisticated works of the Renaissance, art has always been a reflection of our thoughts, emotions, and surroundings. During the Renaissance, art flourished, becoming more detailed and intricate as artists began to merge scientific principles with creative expression. They studied human anatomy, light, depth, and geometry to create paintings that were both appealing and lifelike. With the rise of modern art, the focus shifted toward hidden messages, imbuing artworks with a sense of mystery and discovery. But how can a simple mix of colors and shapes wield such profound influence?

Art conveys messages through visual elements, symbolism, emotion, and historical context. The visual components of color, form, shape, texture, lines, and composition work together to evoke responses from viewers. Each element communicates an emotion or idea, often subconsciously. For example, colors are linked to specific feelings—red may signify passion or aggression, blue can evoke serenity or sadness, and purple often represents royalty or luxury. Artists carefully select their palettes to express particular moods and feelings.

Lines in art also tell stories. Sharp, angular lines may convey tension or aggression, while curved lines suggest gentleness and tranquility. One of the most underrated tools in an artist's repertoire is composition—the arrangement of objects within a painting. A central subject commands attention and importance, while off-centre placements can create a sense of imbalance or chaos.

The expressions with lines and colours

Symbolism plays a significant role in both modern and Renaissance art. By employing historical, personal, or religious icons, artists can express themes that transcend the visual to convey deeper meanings. For instance, a cross may symbolize Christianity, while a lotus flower might represent Eastern philosophies. Van Gogh famously used sunflowers to express gratitude and hope.

Artists are adept at conveying emotion through their work. A chaotic, haphazard drawing can evoke feelings of turbulence, whereas strong, controlled strokes suggest order and stability. Facial expressions, body language, and gestures within a piece communicate stories for viewers to interpret.

Understanding the context and history of a piece can greatly enhance our comprehension of the artist's intent. The events of a particular era shape the art it produces. For example, Renaissance paintings often emphasize religious themes, reflecting the Church's influence and patronage. In contrast, political art, such as Pablo Picasso's *Guernica*, serves as a critique of social issues, often responding to the horrors of war.

Finally, an artist's style carries significant weight. Realism seeks to depict subjects truthfully, making audiences aware of social issues like poverty and hardship. Surrealism presents dreamlike or strange scenes that evoke a sense of fantasy, whimsy, or the unknown.

Impressionism employs loose brushstrokes and light to capture fleeting moments, prioritizing perception over reality.

The world of art is indeed a beautiful and intricate one, rich with layers and meanings. By studying its messages, we can gain deeper insights and appreciation for the complexities of human experience.

67

Why do we sometimes feel happy and sometimes sad?

The Role of Emotions in Human Experience

Emotions play a fundamental role in shaping who we are. They arise from our interactions with the world, conveying our reactions to those around us. Emotions are an integral part of the human experience, but where do they come from, and why do certain things make us happy while others evoke sadness? Let's delve into the science behind our feelings.

Emotions are deeply rooted in our biology, having evolved to help us navigate the world, make decisions, and engage socially. They serve a variety of functions, from basic survival instincts to complex social interactions. Scientifically speaking, all emotions originate in the brain rather than the heart.

Key neurotransmitters, such as serotonin and dopamine, are chemicals that influence our mood by altering the way connections in the brain operate. However, the true regulation of emotions lies within the brain itself. The **amygdala**, located on either side of the brain, processes changes in our emotional environment, particularly those related to fear and threats. The **prefrontal cortex**, located behind the forehead, plays a crucial role in regulating emotional decision-making. Most importantly, the **hypothalamus**, situated above the brainstem, is responsible for our physical reactions to emotions; for example, it increases our heart rate when we experience fear.

The 360 degrees of emotions

When we encounter a stimulus—whether it's a joyful surprise or a startling sound—our brain interprets the situation and triggers the corresponding emotional response. This manifests in physical reactions, such as tears, sweating, or a racing heartbeat, as well as mental experiences like happiness, anger, or fear.

Various hormones and neurotransmitters significantly influence our emotional experiences. Dopamine, associated with pleasure, reward, and motivation, is released when we achieve our goals. Serotonin regulates mood, with low levels linked to sadness and depression.

Cortisol is secreted during times of stress, while oxytocin fosters feelings of trust and love.

These emotions function as an internal feedback system that helps us assess our well-being. We also possess the ability to regulate our emotions. For instance, we may suppress or modify feelings in social contexts, such as remaining calm during a job interview.

Additionally, we can change the way we perceive a stimulus, thereby altering its emotional impact. Viewing mistakes as learning opportunities can help mitigate feelings of disappointment.

It's important to note that emotions are an evolutionary adaptation in humans. They enable quick responses without the need for rationalization. Fear triggers our "fight or flight" response, helping us escape danger, while happiness or excitement encourages us to pursue rewarding behaviors. Disgust prevents us from consuming harmful substances, and feelings of regret reinforce memories to help us avoid similar situations in the future.

Emotions are critical for interpersonal communication. They convey empathy, attachment, and love while also expressing dissatisfaction and displeasure. Our emotions can learn from experiences and significantly influence our decisions. Indeed, we cannot imagine living without them.

68

Why is it fun to play but not to study?

Many of us often feel compelled to work or study, viewing it as a menial chore that detracts from our enjoyment of life. While we recognize the benefits of work and the necessity of study, we frequently find ourselves gravitating toward leisure activities like playing football or scrolling through our phones. So, why do we favor the latter?

The answer lies in how different activities engage our brains and emotions. Play offers a sense of freedom and autonomy, allowing us to choose what we want to do and how we want to do it. In contrast, studying or working requires sustained mental effort and focus, which can place stress on our brains. These tasks often involve reading, manual labor, or repetitive actions that we may not enjoy. If we were required to play every day at 5 a.m., the enjoyment would likely fade, leading to resentment.

A significant factor in this preference is the brain's reward system. Games and enjoyable activities provide immediate satisfaction—whether it's winning a round, solving a puzzle, or simply enjoying the experience. This instant gratification stimulates the brain's reward center, releasing dopamine, a neurotransmitter associated with pleasure and motivation. In contrast, work and study offer delayed gratification; the rewards come much later and require sustained effort. As a result, our brains do not receive the same immediate sense of accomplishment from these tasks.

Working activates the **prefrontal cortex**, the region of the brain responsible for complex cognitive functions such as decision-making, planning, and focus. When we face deadlines and performance pressure, the stress hormone **cortisol** is released, leading to feelings of anxiety and fatigue, which further diminishes our enjoyment of work. In contrast, play encourages exploration, creativity, and novel experiences, which can be inherently rewarding.

All Play and No Work

Our brains have evolved to seek the quickest routes to reward. After completing one experience, they naturally look for the next source of accomplishment. This tendency is rooted in **operant**

conditioning, where behaviors are reinforced by immediate rewards.

Understanding and overcoming this inclination is essential for personal growth and improvement.

Ultimately, recognizing the psychological and emotional dynamics at play can help us find balance between our responsibilities and the joy of leisure activities. By fostering a mindset that values both work and play, we can cultivate a more fulfilling life.

69

Why do leaves change colour?

The Splendor of Autumn: Understanding Tree Changes

Nature's beautiful attire

Autumn, or fall, is one of nature's delights, marked by the crunch of leaves underfoot, a vibrant array of colors, and the gentle sounds of birds returning to roost. The once tall, firm trees that blossomed beautifully in spring now transform into serene shades of brown. But why do they change in this way?

Trees can be classified into two main categories: **deciduous** and **evergreen**. Evergreen trees, typically found in tropical or temperate climates, retain their green leaves throughout the year. In contrast, it is the deciduous trees that dazzle us with their lovely autumn hues before shedding their leaves in winter.

The changing colors of deciduous trees in autumn are primarily due to the breakdown of chlorophyll, the green pigment responsible for the leaves' vibrant color. Chlorophyll enables plants to photosynthesize, converting carbon dioxide into food in the presence of sunlight.

During the spring and summer months, chlorophyll is continuously produced, keeping the leaves green. However, as days grow shorter and temperatures drop, these trees prepare for winter by reducing chlorophyll production, causing the green color to fade and revealing other pigments that were previously masked.

Among these pigments are **carotenoids**, which produce the yellow and orange colors, and **tannins**, which contribute to the brown hues. Some trees also produce **anthocyanins**, pigments that create purples and reds, especially in response to excess sugar. Not all plants produce anthocyanins, which is why only a select few leaves display reddish or purple tones.

But why do deciduous trees shed their leaves in the first place? To survive the harsh conditions of winter, these trees must conserve water and energy. Leaves lose a significant amount of water through transpiration, the process by which moisture escapes from tiny pores (stomata) on their surfaces. As sunlight wanes, temperatures drop, and moisture levels decrease, photosynthesis slows and eventually stops. To protect themselves from water loss and prevent damage from freezing temperatures, deciduous trees drop their leaves, entering a state of dormancy that allows them to conserve resources until spring.

70

How big is the Universe?

The Universe encompasses everything we know and everything we could possibly experience. A vast collection of galaxies with their own stars, planets, and nebulae, it holds both stunning secrets and daunting mysteries. Gazing at the night sky, one might spot the North Star, the planet Venus, or perhaps even a nearby galaxy! Through a professional telescope, more of this celestial grandeur becomes visible: nebulae and clusters come into focus. At the pinnacle of astronomical tools, inventions like the James Webb Telescope reveal the earliest stars and galaxies, captured as breathtaking high-definition images. Looking into the Universe reminds us of its sheer vastness—but just how vast is it?

Before we continue, a gentle warning: this topic might evoke feelings of existential awe. If you're comfortable with that, read on!

The observable Universe is defined as everything we can see from Earth, limited by the time it takes light to travel since the Big Bang. Based on calculations and observations of electromagnetic signals, we estimate that the Universe began 13.8 billion years ago.

However, due to the expansion of space itself, the galaxies that emitted light 13.8 billion years ago are now 46.5 billion light-years (the distance light travels in one year) away from us. So, spanning in all directions, the observable Universe measures approximately 93 billion light-years in diameter.

These numbers are enormous, so let's put them into perspective. One million seconds equals about 12 days, while one billion seconds is 31 years! Ninety-three billion seconds ago, Homer was composing *The Odyssey*. That's just seconds—93 billion years is beyond imagination. For the fastest thing in the Universe (light), it would take 93 billion years to cross the observable Universe. While we know the Universe's size, grasping it conceptually is nearly impossible. And even this is not its end: the real Universe likely extends far beyond what we can observe—a vast, unknowable expanse beyond the cosmic horizon, which marks the point after which light has yet to reach us.

It's worth noting that the Universe is still expanding. Shortly after the Big Bang, it experienced a period of rapid expansion called cosmic inflation. In just a fraction of a second, the Universe expanded exponentially, separating regions of space that were once close.

However, the Universe isn't expanding into something—space itself is expanding. Imagine the Universe as the surface of a balloon, with galaxies as dots on its surface. As the balloon inflates, the dots move farther apart, even though they remain stationary on the surface.

Observations indicate that this expansion is accelerating due to a mysterious force called dark energy.

Dark matter and dark energy remain largely unknown to us. Dark matter makes up about 27% of the Universe, and dark energy 68%, leaving only 5% as observable matter and energy!

These mysterious components neither emit nor absorb light, but we know they exist due to their gravitational effects on galaxies and clusters.

So, where does it end? Some theories propose that the Universe beyond the observable portion is infinite, while others suggest it loops back on itself, like a sphere. What we do know is that if dark energy continues to dominate, the Universe will expand indefinitely. Over time, galaxies will drift so far apart that their light will no longer reach us, leaving future observers in a Universe that appears much smaller and emptier.

Where do you start, and where do you go

71

What was the first thing that ever happened?

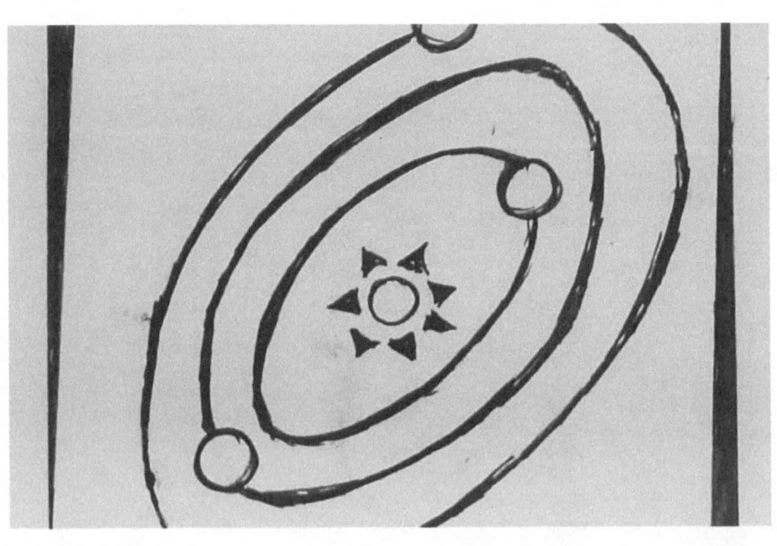

The Genesis

The Beginning of Everything: Cause, Effect, and the Big Bang

We often encounter cause and effect in daily life: because we didn't do our homework, we were scolded by our teacher; because we spent time with a friend, they're now by our side in times of need. All events seem to trace back to something in the past. So, we naturally wonder, "What caused everything to be?"

According to scientific understanding, this "first cause" was the Big Bang, an event that occurred about 13.8 billion years ago. Despite the term, the Big Bang wasn't an explosion but rather the beginning of space and time itself—a silent, rapid expansion from an incredibly dense and hot state.

The first moment after the Big Bang, known as the Planck Epoch (around 10^-43 seconds in), is a time modern physics can barely describe. During this fraction of a second, all fundamental forces—gravity, electromagnetism, strong, and weak nuclear forces—were unified. The Universe was incredibly hot, dense, and dominated by quantum effects. But within the next second, the Universe cooled slightly, allowing the formation of the first building blocks of matter, called quarks.

In this time, the Universe expanded exponentially—space itself stretched faster than the speed of light, causing tiny quantum fluctuations that eventually seeded galaxies. After this rapid inflation, quarks swam freely in a hot "quark-gluon plasma" along with radiation, while the four fundamental forces separated. Eventually, quarks combined to form protons and neutrons, creating the matter that forms the basis of our universe. Interestingly, there was initially equal matter and antimatter, but for reasons still unknown, a slight imbalance favored matter, allowing it to dominate.

Gradually, fundamental particles continued to combine. Light particles, called photons, were present, but free electrons in space blocked them, preventing light from traveling far. Over time, electrons combined with protons and neutrons to form atoms, allowing light to travel freely and beginning the observable Universe as we know it.

Asking what happened "before" the Big Bang is challenging since time itself began with it. Without time, the concept of "before" doesn't apply in the traditional sense. Though theories like the multiverse or a cyclical universe remain intriguing, they're impossible to confirm at this stage. We must be content with our current understanding and accept that time itself was born from the Big Bang.

72

How do fish breathe underwater?

Life under Water

Life Underwater: The Survival Secrets of Fish

Fish are fascinating creatures. Unlike land animals, which experience the wind, sun, and stars, fish, whales, and sharks live in an entirely different world. But how do they survive? How do they breathe, sleep, and eat?

Sleeping Patterns

Fish don't sleep the way land animals do. They don't have eyelids to close, and they don't lie down. Instead, fish enter restful periods of reduced activity. During this time, they slow their metabolism and remain still, often settling near a shelter on the pond or ocean floor. However, they stay alert to any threats, ready to move if needed. This state of restful vigilance allows them to recharge while remaining safe from potential dangers.

Diets and Eating Habits

Fish diets vary widely depending on their species and habitat. Some fish are carnivores, feasting on other fish, shrimp, crabs, or insects. Others are herbivores, grazing on algae or aquatic plants like duckweed. Many fish are omnivores, consuming a combination of plants and animals. This diversity in diet allows fish to thrive in nearly all aquatic environments.

Breathing Mechanism

The underwater breathing process in fish relies on specialized organs called gills. Gills enable them to extract oxygen from water and expel carbon dioxide, functioning similarly to human lungs. Each gill is made up of thin, feathery structures known as gill filaments, densely packed with blood vessels to increase surface area for gas exchange.

To breathe, fish open their mouths, drawing water in. The water flows over their gills and exits through the operculum, a bony cover on each side of the head. As water moves over the gill filaments, oxygen diffuses into the fish's bloodstream, and carbon dioxide diffuses out.

Fish have evolved a remarkable mechanism called "countercurrent exchange." Blood in the gills flows in the opposite direction to the incoming water, ensuring that oxygen moves efficiently from the water into the bloodstream by maintaining a steep concentration gradient.

Most fish use a technique called *buccal pumping*, actively pushing water over their gills using their throat muscles. Some species, like sharks and tuna, use *ram ventilation*, which involves swimming with their mouths open to push water through their gills. These species must keep moving to breathe and risk suffocation if they stop!

Through these efficient adaptations, fish have evolved a unique way to thrive underwater, revealing how the physics of gas diffusion plays a fundamental role in sustaining an entire kingdom of life.

73

Why can't we see air?

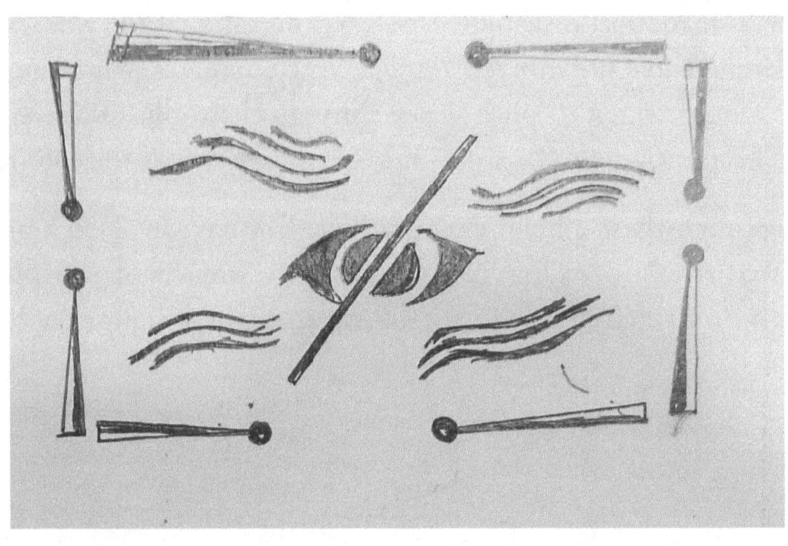

The visible invisible

The Mystery of Transparency: Why Some Things Are Invisible

Transparent materials can be puzzling. We've all seen videos of people walking straight into glass doors or windows. And although we know air is all around us, we can't actually see it moving. Why do these materials appear invisible to us?

It all comes down to how light interacts with different substances. Visible light consists of a spectrum of colors known as VIBGYOR – violet, indigo, blue, green, yellow, orange, and red. Everything we see is a combination of these colors, and the way an object appears depends on how it interacts with light.

Objects are made of atoms, and each atom contains one or more electrons that orbit its nucleus. These electrons aren't free to move just anywhere; they're limited to certain energy levels, or "orbits." While an electron can jump from one level to another, it can only do so by absorbing a specific amount of energy. For instance, an electron may have energies of 13.6 eV or 3.4 eV, but it can't possess a value between them.

Why does this matter for visibility? Well, light also carries energy. When light of a particular frequency (or color) hits an electron, it transfers its energy to the electron, allowing it to jump to a higher level. After a brief stay at this higher level, the electron "falls" back down, releasing light of the same frequency that it absorbed. This emitted light is what gives objects their color. For example, we see white when all colors of light are absorbed and re-emitted together.

But transparent materials, like air and glass, behave differently. The electrons in these materials don't have energy levels that match the energy of visible light photons. As a result, visible light passes through them without being absorbed. Since the light moves through unchanged, it carries with it the visual information of everything on the other side. Our eyes perceive this, making us largely unaware of the transparent material in front of us – unless, of course, there's a smudge or fingerprint on the glass to give it away.

74

How does a camera capture what it sees?

The Wonder of the Camera: How Moments Are Captured

A camera is a marvelous invention, preserving memories that might otherwise fade with time. It allows us to hold onto slices of life and revisit moments of joy, amazement, or warmth whenever we choose. But how exactly does a camera capture the world around us?

At its core, a camera works by recording light from any object in front of it to produce an image. The process begins with the camera's most crucial part: the lens. The lens gathers and focuses light from the scene onto an image sensor or, in older models, onto photographic film. As light passes through the lens, it converges toward a point known as the focus. The distance between the lens and this focus point is called the focal length, while the size of the lens opening is called the aperture. By adjusting these two settings, a camera can alter the field of view and depth of an image. A larger aperture lets in more light, while a longer focal length provides a magnified view of the scene.

The shutter plays another key role by controlling the duration of exposure—the length of time light is allowed to reach the sensor. A fast shutter speed freezes motion, whereas a slower speed introduces motion blur, giving images a sense of movement.

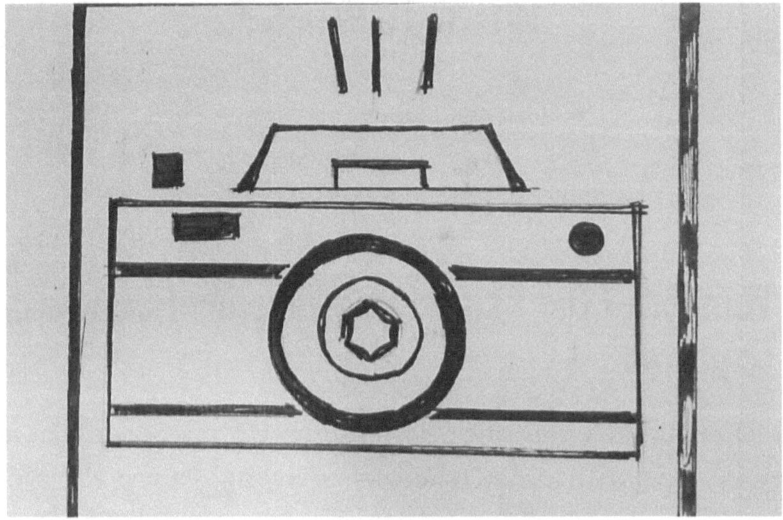

The clicking shutter

Modern cameras use image sensors to transform captured light into electrical signals. These sensors consist of pixels, each representing a specific area of the scene. The sensor records both the intensity and frequency of light on each pixel, which translates into brightness and color in the final image. While digital cameras convert light to electronic signals, traditional film cameras rely on a chemical process. In film cameras, light exposure activates chemicals on the film, gradually building up an image that reflects the scene's brightness and color.

Though the processes differ, both digital and film cameras capture scenes by exposing specific areas to light and recording intensity and frequency. Digital sensors capture this data through light-sensitive receptors that convert light energy into electrical signals, whereas film cameras achieve it through chemical reactions. Both methods let us hold onto moments, ensuring they're always within reach.

75

Is there life on another planet?

The Search for Life Beyond Earth

Life is one of the world's precious mysteries. How did we come to be? Did a higher power create us? These are questions that spark both curiosity and awe. In our search for companionship, humanity has turned its gaze outward, seeking signs of life in the cosmos.

Thousands of exoplanets—planets that orbit stars outside our solar system—have been discovered. For an exoplanet to have even a chance of hosting life, it must meet certain conditions. Firstly, it should lie within the "Goldilocks zone," the ideal range from a star where temperatures are just right—not too hot, nor too cold—for liquid water to exist. Water, as we know, is essential for life. Additionally, the exoplanet needs a stable atmosphere with essential gases, such as oxygen or carbon dioxide. By analyzing light and radiation from these planets and comparing them with known refraction patterns of various gases, scientists can deduce the chemical composition of their atmospheres.

Beyond these requirements, life-friendly planets benefit from geological processes that recycle nutrients, a magnetic field to shield against solar radiation, and a stable host star. While a handful of exoplanets meet these criteria, we have yet to find definitive evidence of life on any of them.

Who is my counter-part beyond my planet

Life on Earth, however, has proven resilient in extreme environments, thriving in acidic lakes, hydrothermal vents, and other inhospitable locations. This resilience has inspired us to look within our own solar system for potential life. Mars, for instance, has shown signs that it once held conditions suitable for life, including evidence of ancient water, seasonal methane emissions, and subsurface ice. Similarly, the icy moons Europa and Enceladus may harbor life in the oceans beneath their frozen crusts.

Given the vastness of the universe—with billions of galaxies and potentially trillions of planets—many scientists believe it is statistically probable that life exists elsewhere. Yet, while we continue to search, the discovery of intelligent life remains an unanswered question.

76

What's a black hole? The Enigma of Black Holes

The mysteries of the Universe are vast and awe-inspiring, yet no cosmic entity fills us with more dread than a black hole. The deep, resonant sounds of a black hole, as released by NASA, add to its dark allure. But what exactly are these hauntingly majestic phenomena?

A black hole is a region in space where gravity is so powerful that nothing—not even light— can escape it. This is puzzling since gravity traditionally acts only on objects with mass, and light particles are massless. So how can a black hole trap light? Instead of pulling in matter in a conventional sense, a black hole warps the very fabric of space, creating a zone where all directions lead inward. This remarkable and terrifying nature is rooted in the theory of General Relativity.

So, how do black holes form? When a massive star runs out of nuclear fuel, it collapses under its own gravity in a spectacular supernova explosion. If the remaining mass is sufficient, it compresses into a black hole. A black hole comprises two main parts: the event horizon and the singularity. The event horizon is the boundary that marks the "point of no return." Beyond this boundary, nothing can escape the black hole's grip. At its core lies the singularity, a theoretical point where gravity becomes infinitely strong and space-time curves infinitely.

The conditions at this singularity are so extreme that they lie beyond the scope of our current understanding of physics.

Since light cannot escape a black hole, how do we even know they exist? We detect black holes through their gravitational effects. When matter is drawn toward a black hole, it often forms an intensely hot, spinning disk called an accretion disk. As the material in this disk accelerates, it heats up and emits detectable X-rays. Additionally, the orbits of stars and gas clouds around an invisible spot in space can indicate the presence of a black hole.

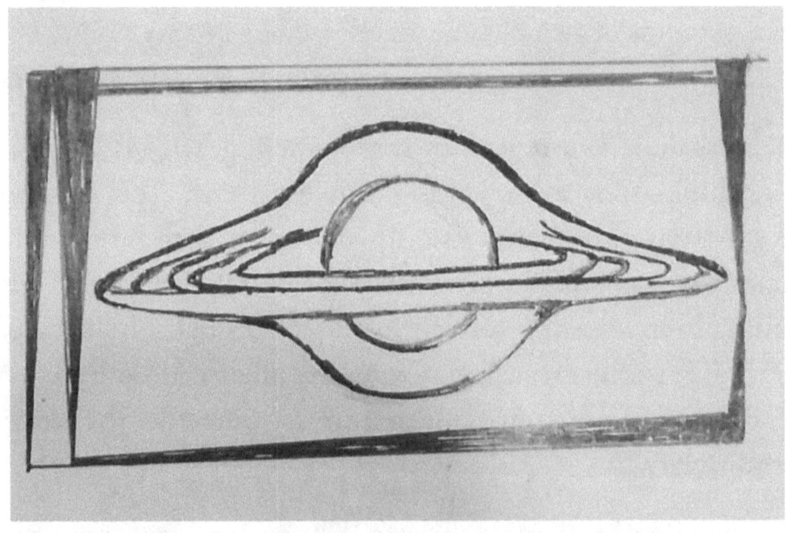

The inexorable force in the Cosmos

One intriguing question often asked is what would happen if someone fell into a black hole. Imagine an astronaut drifting towards one. As they near the event horizon, the difference in gravitational force between their head and feet would stretch their body in a process called "spaghettification" (not an ideal way to grow taller!). Once they cross the event horizon, they reach the point of no return. Time itself would distort, and they would experience a vastly different flow of time, though from their perspective, they'd seem to continue falling forever.

Finally, the ultimate mystery lies in the singularity, where all known physical laws break down. While we cannot know what happens there, black holes continue to challenge our understanding of the Universe.

For a compelling exploration of these ideas, I'd highly recommend watching *Interstellar*, a film that dives into these cosmic mysteries with remarkable creativity.

77

How do bees make honey?

The undiluted natural sweetness

Honey: A Timeless Treasure

Honey has been cherished by humans for centuries. Ancient civilizations such as the Egyptians, Greeks, and Romans relished it in their desserts. Not only is honey a natural and healthy sweetener, but when stored properly, it also has an incredible shelf life—natural honey kept in a solid form and well-preserved can remain edible indefinitely. Archaeologists have even discovered perfectly preserved honey in sealed pots from Ancient Egyptian tombs.

But the process of honey production is far more complex than its sweetness suggests! Honeybees craft honey with remarkable efficiency, beginning by collecting nectar from flowers. This nectar, a sugary liquid produced by flowers to attract pollinators, is drawn up by the bees' long, tube-like tongues called proboscises. The nectar is then stored in a specialized part of the bee's body known as the honey stomach, which is distinct from its regular stomach. Inside this honey stomach, the nectar mixes with enzymes like invertase, which begin breaking down complex sugars.

Once a bee returns to its hive, it regurgitates the partially processed nectar and passes it on to another worker bee in a process called trophallaxis, or mouth-to-mouth transfer. This exchange occurs several times, with each bee breaking down the sugars even further. Finally, the processed nectar is placed into a honeycomb cell within the hive. The bees then fan the nectar with their wings to evaporate water, thickening it into honey. Once the nectar is sufficiently dehydrated, it's sealed with a layer of beeswax, and the honey continues to mature. With its low water and high sugar content, honey naturally resists fermentation.

Honey serves as an essential food reserve for bees, providing them with energy, especially in the winter months. This natural process of preservation has allowed humans to benefit from its sweetness and health benefits for centuries.

78

What causes thunder and lightning?

The Thrill of a Thunderstorm

I recall a late afternoon when the sky took on an ominous shade of grey. Within minutes, the gentle pitter-patter on my windowsill escalated into a full downpour. Suddenly, a flash of lightning lit up my room, casting shadows across the walls. I glanced at my watch, and, sure enough, within five seconds, a rumbling thunder shook the building. I sat there amidst the calming din of the rain, feeling the thrill and tranquility only a thunderstorm could bring. This experience left me pondering the origins of such powerful displays. After some research, here's what I found.

Thunder and lightning are part of the same natural phenomenon, two sides of the same coin. Inside a thundercloud, regions become electrically charged due to the interaction of water droplets, ice particles, and air currents. Typically, the top of the cloud becomes positively charged while the bottom becomes negatively charged. This difference creates a strong potential gradient, generating an electric field. When the field becomes intense enough, it results in a sudden discharge of electricity, releasing electrons. This discharge can occur within the cloud, between clouds, or even between the cloud and the ground—the latter being the most dramatic form we observe, known as cloud-to-ground lightning. Once the discharge reaches the ground, a powerful electric current called the return stroke surges back up, creating the bright flash of lightning we see.

The heat produced by lightning can reach temperatures around 30,000 degrees Celsius— much hotter than the surface of the Sun! This extreme heat causes the surrounding air to expand rapidly, creating a shockwave. This shockwave is what we hear as thunder.

Lightning and Thunder — Rocking in Wonder

While the entire phenomenon occurs almost instantaneously, we perceive lightning before we hear thunder. This difference underscores the varying speeds of light and sound. Light travels nearly a million times faster than sound, reaching our eyes almost instantly, whereas sound takes longer to reach our ears, causing a delay of about five seconds per mile. In fact, you can estimate the distance of a lightning strike by counting the seconds between the flash and the sound of thunder: every five seconds of delay translates to roughly one mile away.

79

Why do diamonds sparkle?

Diamonds are precious jewels that have become symbols of elegance, often gracing engagement rings and enhancing one's look with their timeless sparkle. While diamond jewelry may lack vibrant colors, it more than makes up for this with an unmatched brilliance. But what gives diamonds their unique, dazzling shimmer?

Typically, light travels in a straight line until it encounters a new medium, where it is either reflected or refracted. Reflection occurs when light bounces off a surface, while refraction happens when light enters a new medium and bends due to the difference in speeds between the two materials. You can imagine it like a car driving from sand onto concrete at an angle— if one wheel hits the concrete first, it speeds up, causing the car to turn before fully straightening out on the new surface. This analogy offers a simple way to understand refraction, though light doesn't behave exactly like a car.

So, what does this mean for diamonds? The magic lies in how light behaves when moving from a slower medium (like diamond) to a faster one (like air). As light exits the diamond, it bends sharply toward the surface. If it hits the surface at a specific angle or higher, known as the critical angle, it cannot escape. Instead, it reflects back into the diamond. This phenomenon is called ***total internal reflection***, and it's central to a diamond's sparkle.

Diamonds have a small critical angle, which means light entering them is easily trapped and bounces multiple times within the stone before eventually escaping. This repeated internal reflection makes the light appear more intense and gives diamonds their characteristic shimmer, capturing our attention with each brilliant facet.

The Rare Sparkle

80

Why do onions make us cry?

Chopping onions can feel like a daunting task. At first, it seems manageable—the fine dicing being the only hurdle. But within minutes, our eyes start to sting, and tears flow like a waterfall. With blurry vision, we push through until all the onions are finely chopped, but the irritation lingers. So, why do onions do this? Do they have a personal vendetta against us?

Onions belong to the Allium family, which includes garlic, leeks, and shallots. These plants absorb sulfur from the soil and use it to produce defensive chemicals. Inside the onion's cells, there are compartments that store sulfur-containing compounds, specifically S-1-propenyl-L- cysteine sulfoxide. These compounds, along with an enzyme called alliinase, are theorized to serve as a defense mechanism against animals, insects, and fungi, as well as to protect the plant from pathogens.

When we cut into an onion, we break open those cells, causing the sulfoxides and enzymes to mix. This initiates a series of chemical reactions. The enzyme converts the sulfoxides into sulphenic acid, which quickly transforms into syn-Propanethial-S-oxide. This highly reactive compound is responsible for our tears. The gas released comes into contact with the surface of our eyes, which are coated in a thin layer of moisture. This interaction produces sulfuric acid, irritating the nerve endings in our eyes. As a response, the lacrimal glands (the tear- making glands) are triggered to flush away the irritant. Unfortunately, as we continue chopping, more of the gas is produced, perpetuating the cycle.

Is there a way to mitigate this tearful reaction? Thankfully, there are a few tricks! Chilling the onion slows down the reaction between the enzyme and the sulfur compounds. Cutting an onion underwater prevents the gas from reaching our eyes, and using a sharper knife causes less damage to the onion cells, thereby reducing the amount of irritant released.

I can't do without onions, even though I cry

81

How do I keep learning?

Learning is a Never-Ending Journey!

Embrace curiosity and keep an open mind, and knowledge will flow naturally. Enjoy the process of learning every day, right up to your last day!

My promise to my parents — I will learn every day

www.ingramcontent.com/pod-product-compliance
Lightning Source LLC
LaVergne TN
LVHW041158150826
845673LV00001B/205

* 9 7 9 8 8 9 6 1 0 7 0 2 6 *